GATHER THE OUTCASTS
Reaching the Lost in Africa

God Bless You!
Psalm 37:4

James Rowh

Advanced Global Publishing
P.O. Box 310, Shippensburg, PA 17257-0310

ISBN 13 Trade Paper: 978-0-7684-0938-3
ISBN 13 E-book: 978-0-7684-0939-0

For Worldwide Distribution, Printed in the U.S.A.
3 4 5 6 7 8 9 10 11 / 20 19 18 17

TABLE OF CONTENTS

INTRODUCTION

The following is a narrative of stories and events that took place in Africa from the year 2009 until 2014. All of the stories are true, I have brought them to life on the pages of this book to the best of my recollection, as very few of them were written down or kept in a journal prior to this writing. I have been given the awesome privilege of being a servant for the Lord; He alone gets the glory for all the amazing things that have happened over there. I pray that you will meet Him in the pages of this book.

Gather the Outcasts Ministry dates back to 2001, and began as a prison ministry. I talk a bit about that in the narrative, but this book primarily focuses on the Africa missions. All the names of the people in this book have been changed for their protection and privacy. May God bless you as you read, and I hope you enjoy seeing Africa through the lens of Gather the Outcasts Ministry.

CHAPTER 1

The Dream 2009

I awoke from a deep sleep with a start, looked at the clock and the time was three in the morning. I knew I had just been given a dream, and as I lay still in a state of half-sleep, half-awake, I drifted back into the dream and began to record the details in my mind. What did it mean? Was it a profound spiritual dream from the Lord, or just another of a series of dreams with no particular impact? As I focused more on the details, after a few minutes I felt I had them secure enough to get up and write a narrative of the dream.

As my mind cleared and I began to write, I realized the dream was a significant spiritual dream, one of those dreams that can reveal a person's destiny. In the dream, I was standing on a platform, a rather large platform, like the kind I had seen in revival crusade settings. I was standing behind a podium, and in my right hand I was holding a Bible, high up in the air over my head, my New American Standard Study Bible that I have had for about thirty years, a very familiar Bible to me primarily because it is large and quite heavy. In my left hand I was holding a large, white bag that was full of ear corn; the front of the bag had written on it in large, black letters, the following words: REVELATION 22. I knew, of course, this was the last book of the Bible, but it was quite perplexing in the place and way in which it was written.

Behind me on the platform was a large grain bin, holding approximately two thousand bushels of ear corn, the old type of wooden slat bin that was a familiar site on farmsteads all over the Midwest many years ago. In the bin was ear corn, full ears twelve to fifteen inches long, and the bin was full clear to the top, right to the roof of the bin. Out in front of me were thousands of black people listening to the message that I was preaching from the platform, and between me and the black people was a rather curious line of men, about forty in number, standing in a line facing the crowds. The men all had similar dress; blue jeans, with blue denim shirts, and red baseball hats.

As I wrote the details of the dream down, I began to ponder on the meaning of it all. What was the Lord attempting to show me? I prayed that night before I went back to sleep, and then the next morning prayed again for the Lord to show me the interpretation of the dream. Over the next few days, the meaning of the dream began to unfold to me. The Lord was showing me I was going to be preaching in Africa, as those out in front of the platform were unmistakably African people; the dark black complexion with all the bright colored clothing, the people were easy to identify against a backdrop of the pitch black African sky.

The men in line between me and the African people were men from the prison where I preach on a regular basis – they were dressed in their typical prison uniform of blues and red hats, I recognized them immediately. Since they were between me and the people receiving the message, I believe the Lord was showing me they were going to be my intercessors, the intermediaries who would stand in the gap for me when I was away on the mission field. I mused at the proficiency of the Lord. He always makes the most use of the resources at hand, who better to be the prayer warriors for the mission than those men in the prison who have time to pray, time to study their Bibles, time to fast and intercede. The interpretation of the image of me on the platform was a bit more complex, so I continued to seek the Lord in prayer, and He kept unfolding the meaning to me in bits and pieces.

The message coming from me was unmistakable; it was coming directly from the Word of God, in my right hand, the hand of strength, the hand of power. In my left hand, the white bag with the words "Revelation 22," God was showing me I was going to be giving the message of the good news of the gospel, the hope for all eternity, the message of the New Jerusalem coming down out of heaven, described in great detail in the last book of the Bible, Revelation 22. The bag was full of ear corn, the same type of white ears of corn that filled the slat bin behind me on the platform; the Lord was showing me that He was going to be my provision, Jehovah Jireh, the Lord of Provision. The provision was going to be there for my every need and every mission trip to Africa, it would be there in bulk storage in the big bin, and be there in the small amounts in each and every setting where I would need it, as symbolized by the white bag full of ear corn.

As I wrote the interpretation down, I pondered the meaning, as many of God's servants have done throughout the recorded history of the Bible, when they had an encounter with God and it left them in awe, and in many cases reeling. I had no particular attachment to Africa, or that it would even be on my radar in any particular way. Why Africa? Why me? My resume, from my point of view, was pretty weak. I had been preaching for many years in a state run prison facility not far from my home, and over the years had preached many voluntary callouts there, and in the summer many big yard revival events out in the open air plaza at the prison. And I had made several short term mission sojourns into Mexico to build houses for the poor of Jaurez, along the way gaining some very valuable experience in relating to people of different cultures, and certainly different economic status.

In addition to that, from 2006 to 2009 I made three trips to Costa Rica to minister to the Cabecar indigenous people of southern Costa Rica, a remote tribe of indigenous who were chased up into the mountains by the Spanish four hundred years ago and left to fend for themselves as time gradually passed them by. The Cabecar were passed by and forgotten for nearly four hundred years, not even counted as people for all those years and even today are certainly considered to be on the outskirts of civil society in Costa Rica. They certainly fit the description of the outcasts. Just getting back into the rugged mountains they call home, now their reservation, is a strenuous task, not to mention having to pack in all the necessary provisions for a stay of any length. The village that we packed into was a half day journey over the steepest mountain trails imaginable, and then at the bottom of the trail came the crossing of a rushing, wild river, the Chirropo, that often was impossible to cross on foot.

So I had some experiences and opportunities serving the Lord in bringing in the outcasts of the nations into His kingdom. Those kingdom opportunities were invaluable in learning to be obedient to the Lord, to listen for His voice, to seek His wisdom and counsel in every situation and decision. But Africa, why there, and why me, and why now? Africa seemed to me to be so remote, so far away, the place of witchcraft, and in recent years, terrorist bombings, but also a place of great missionary stories, miracles, signs, and wonders. It was all a bit overwhelming as I thought about how I was to fit into all of it. As I do with all the prophetic dreams the Lord has given me, I wrote it all down in my dream journal and shelved it on the top shelf of my spiritual closet, and then I began to pray for the Lord to take me to the next step, to nurture the dream.

God was beginning to reveal to me in a deeper way the meaning of the term "Gather the Outcasts," the name He had given me for the ministry back in 2001. The phrase, "Gather the Outcasts," came from a passage of Scripture that had jumped out at me one morning when I was reading through the Bible. In Micah, the Lord speaks through the prophet Micah, and He speaks about the end time Millennial reign of Jesus by saying, "In that day," says the Lord, "*I will assemble the lame, I will gather the outcast and those whom I have afflicted; I will make the lame a remnant, and the outcast a strong nation; So the Lord will reign over them in Mount Zion from now on, even forever.*" (Micah 4:6,7)

The idea that the Lord was going to gather all the lame and the outcasts and make them a strong nation really struck a spiritual cord with me, and as I prayed about it, the Lord confirmed it in many ways. Prison ministry, what is that but gathering the outcasts? The tattoos, the long hair, missing teeth from drug abuse, scars from fights, rough men who had grown up on the streets and the fringes of lawful society, the forgotten and the left behind, God had over the years given me a passion to love these men.

When the Lord first started to speak to me about the name Gather the Outcasts, I had no idea of the places that He wanted to take me; to the Cabecar Reservation, the Navajo Reservation, into the poorest places of the world, the slums of Juarez, the slums of Kibera in Nairobi, and on over to the poorest of the poor in Uganda and the Democratic

Republic of the Congo. By the year 2010, I was beginning to see a pattern in all this; that God was sending me into some of the more difficult places to reach the lost, those whom societies had rejected and were deemed unlovable and not worth the effort to go get for the kingdom of God. But I struggled with the name. I wanted something warm and fuzzy, something that had an easy ring and hook to it, and so I argued a bit with the Lord about the name. But Gather the Outcasts gradually stayed with me, the Lord had His way. Little did I know of the truth of that name, as I peered into the prophetic future the Lord had destined for me.

CHAPTER 2

The Call

I was working at my natural foods store in the spring of 2010, it was a few months after I had received the prophetic dream. Though cognizant of the dream, it wasn't something I was thinking about that day, as the pressures of running a small business and an organic farm were foremost on my plate for that day. Then I received a phone call from an evangelist friend, brother Daniel, who was calling to tell me about an opportunity he had been given to go with a large group from Washington state, who were going to Kenya to minister in the Nairobi area. The purpose of the trip was twofold: to minister the good news of the gospel to the poor in the Nairobi area, primarily in the area of the Kibera slum, a giant slum that is home to half a million people, many of whom subsist on fifty cents a day, and secondly to visit children in some of the orphanages in the Kibera area. The group consisted of about eighteen people total, half of whom were part of a magnificent praise and worship team, the other half support personnel for the band, and others who were primarily going for the orphan ministry team.

As Daniel related this mission to me, he asked me a question that sort of stunned me, but at the same time excited me very much. "Jim, would you be interested in going along with this group to Kenya, they need some preachers to go with them to preach in the churches and the revivals that will be held during the week?" As I listened to his words, the prophetic dream, the vision of me standing on the platform, holding up my Bible in one hand and a bag of corn in the other, speaking to a crowd of African people who were standing out in an open field to hear the word, all those images came rushing back to me. Without any prayer or hesitation I said, "Yes, I would be interested in going, get me the details of the trip and let me know when they are going."

The Lord had prepared my heart and given me a desire to go, so when the open door came I didn't have to think about it long, or spend any time in prayer, all that had already been done. A call came later in the week regarding the details of the mission, the amount of support money needed, and who all would be going. I was signed on and things were moving fast, preparations were being made, a team was coming together; ten musicians and tech people comprised the worship team, five ladies who would be primarily ministering in the orphanages, three preachers, and one mission administrator. We were scheduled for departure in late July, and the excitement was starting to build!

CHAPTER 3

Intercessor's Vision

As the time for the departure to Kenya quickly arrived, I had been exhorting the inmates in the prison where I preach on a weekly basis, asking them to spend time in prayer and fasting for the necessary provision for the mission, not only for myself but for the team as a whole. Each person going was to raise three thousand dollars for their own personal travel funds, which was to include money for a three day visit to the Maasai Mara Wildlife Refuge in southern Kenya. In addition to the individual provision necessary, the team as a whole had budgeted thirty thousand dollars to raise to pay for all the sound systems, the platform construction, security, transportation, and advertising for a week of small crusades to be held at various parks and open space venues all over Nairobi.

The week of evangelism would culminate in the grand finale, the All Church Picnic, to be held in Uhuru Park in central Nairobi at the end of the week of praise and worship and preaching in the smaller venues. So a lot of money needed to be raised in a fairly short amount of time; in addition, I asked to inmates to spend time in prayer for the success of the mission, that many would hear the Word, many would receive healing and deliverance from the Lord, and many would respond by making a life changing salvation decision.

The last night in the prison a group of about twenty five inmates and myself were down on our knees, seeking the Lord and crying out to Him for all those needs, both known and unknown, that a mission of this nature and size would require. After praying for about thirty minutes, one of the inmate brothers, a brother Patrick, came up to me and said, " Jim, the Lord just gave me a vision of you ministering to a lady who is severely demon oppressed, and she is coming to be set free from the life of torment she is in. In addition to all that, when she comes to you, she will be holding a small child, and the Lord is saying to me that I am to pray for that child all the rest of my life."

As I listened to him describe that vision for me, all I could do was mutter, "Wow, that is quite a vision the Lord is giving you." And we both nodded in agreement, as it was becoming increasingly clear that the prophetic dream given to me about the inmates being the intercessors for the mission was going to be fulfilled in ways that neither I nor they had ever imagined. Later, when we got to Nairobi, I encountered the lady that brother Patrick had seen in his vision, but it wasn't until the end of the week when we got to the Uhuru Park Crusade, which I'll talk about when sharing about all the ministry events of the time we were in Nairobi.

CHAPTER 4

On to Nairobi!

After driving to Denver and then catching a flight from Denver to Detroit, brother Daniel and I met up in Detroit. From there we flew to Amsterdam, had a few hour layover to catch a short nap, then we were on our way on an eight hour flight to Nairobi, where we were to meet up with the rest of the team flying in from Washington state. We arrived in Nairobi on a balmy July night about nine, and after standing in line for an hour with the other three hundred people who were on the plane to purchase Kenya visas, we were met by our Kenyan hosts. The sights, sounds, and smells of Nairobi were overwhelming to the senses, a bit like seeing the ocean for the very first time. The sights that particularly stood out to me were the smiling faces of the Kenyan hosts, their smiling faces and color so black against the background of the black African night; the trash of Nairobi, plastic bags and trash piles everywhere I looked; the potholes in the roads, even the main road leading to and from the Kenyatta International Airport, as if to say, "We don't intend to impress, this is Africa!"

The sounds come from a city of four million inhabitants, a bustling financial center with bumper to bumper "jam," that is to say traffic jam, in which everyone is seemingly trying to get to the same place at the same time. All of them rely heavily on laying on their horn, cutting across shortcuts, including down in the road ditches and through gas station parking lots, driving in the opposing lane of oncoming traffic for as far as one can get away with, until someone comes from the other direction to force the issue. All those sounds formed the melody of Nairobi. The sounds also included diesel trucks shifting gears, slamming on the brakes, radios sometimes blaring a mix of gospel music, American pop music, and African music. And then there are the matatus, the lories or mini buses, where the barkers are hanging out the door of the bus at every intersection, trying to entice riders, or banging on the roof of the bus to let the driver know to stop or it was all right to proceed.

The smells of humans, millions all packed together in a very small area, as everywhere I looked there was people, people, people. It was quite the opposite of what I was used to in Western Kansas, where the little village where my farm is located has only thirty residents, and the county seat town, the largest town in the county, has only three thousand residents. Nairobi, the home of burning trash piles, where people light fires in every neighborhood to stay warm on the chilly nights, and also where the big ears of corn are roasted and sold to passersby on many street corners all over the city. Where the outdoor food vendors are heating up charcoal grills to fry fish, just transported in from Lake Victoria or from Mombasa on the sea coast, or to grill chicken breasts or roast whole chickens on outdoor rotisseries in front of pubs and discos. So when you mix all that together, the sights, the sounds, the smells, the senses are screaming out, this is going to be an unmistakable adventure worth every minute of the prayer, the fasting , the money raising, and yes, the anxiety and anticipation of something never before experienced.

Brother Daniel and I were in Nairobi for a couple of days, staying with a local pastor and his family, and then we joined up with the main team from Washington, where we were lodged at Africa Nazarene University on the outskirts of Nairobi. After getting to know each other for a day or so, we were ready to tackle the mission head on; to preach the gospel from the back of a big flatbed truck, outfitted with a monster sound system that would blare out worship music and the good news of the gospel into every park and open space where we would stop for a couple hours. We would also preach in churches that had invited us in to preach at the noon time prayer and worship sessions that many churches in the Nairobi area conduct.

And in addition to all that, some of the team were visiting orphanages and playing with the children, and visiting neighborhoods with the idea of finding places to set up micro business enterprises, such as sewing and designing garments to sell for a profit. All of this activity was a prelude to the climax at the end of the week with the big All Church Picnic, the crusade in Uhuru Park in central Nairobi, where, hopefully, all the people touched during the week would come out for a big grand finale, praise and worship and preaching fest.

CHAPTER 5

Kibera

My first preaching assignment was in a small church in Kibera, preaching to a gathering of the Kibera Pastor's Association. The church building was crude as many are in Africa, a basic pole structure covered with sheet metal, dirty cement floor, with a barely functioning sound system, with just enough volume to cover the thirty by fifty foot structure. This was a gathering of about sixty pastors, men and women who all had churches in the big slum of Kibera, a place three hundred thousand, some say half a million, people call home. A place of unbelievable poverty, orphan children, HIV/AIDS and many other medical clinics, as well as open displays of all the wretchedness of abject poverty; prostitution, teenagers sniffing glue and other chemicals in plastic soda bottles, rows and acres of sheet metal huts all crammed together with no space in between, most less than ten feet square. Alongside many of the pathways, open streams of human urine and excrement flowed to who knows where.

The people of Kibera survive on less than a dollar a day on the average, and since it is a squatter's slum, the people own no land. Since they have no rights or services provided by the government, the tends to stay in the state of poverty that they are in, as it is quite convenient for the government to say, "Hands off, we don't owe the residents of Kibera anything, and therefore, they have no right to expect anything." Because people of Kibera survive on so little money each day, it is often the first place that immigrants from the rural areas of Kenya, and other countries in East Africa, land when they come to Nairobi to try and improve their lot in life over the poverty of many of the rural areas of Africa. So the flow is rural poverty to urban poverty, with little if any improvement. I'm sure the typical attitude of the immigrant is this: at least in Kibera if we are dirt poor, we will have the bright lights of the city, and lots of other Kenyans to keep us company while we attempt to scratch out a living. Many land in Kibera thinking it will just be a temporary stopping place, but find out it becomes a place of grinding, gripping poverty that has a life and breath all its own, and doesn't let its residents go away easily or without a fight.

And so the ten thousands became one hundred thousand, the hundred thousand became two hundred, and now three hundred, and some say even half a million call Kibera home. And if you tally up the number in the Mathare slum and other slums in Nairobi, all almost within the shadows cast by the big banks and hotels of downtown Nairobi, a huge percentage of the people living in this financial capital of East Africa, are actually living in wretched slums. The contrast between the haves and have nots in Nairobi is quite startling and shocking to say the least.

A team of four of us went to Kibera for a noontime meeting, and as the sixty or so pastors took their seats, I had nothing but admiration for them and for the tough job they had been called to do. To minister in a place like Kibera would take a lot of perseverance, a lot of submission to the Lord, a lot of picking up one's cross and carrying it daily. It would not be an easy call; the money and perks would be practically nonexistent, the spiritual warfare battles against the addictions, the drugs and alcohol, the glue sniffing, the rampant sexual immorality, all of that would be depressing enough; but then in addition to that throw in the battles against witchcraft, Islam, and other pagan religions would be enough to wear down even the most zealous of the Lord's servants.

As I stood at the podium to preach, to give the pastor's a word of encouragement, I had a message from the book of Acts to impart to them. "Men of Israel, listen to these words: Jesus the Nazarene, a man attested to you by God with miracles and wonders and signs which God performed through Him in your midst, just as you yourselves know…..' (Acts 2:22) I was just beginning to preach the message when the Holy Spirit gave me a word of knowledge about some of the pastors in the room, a word which I instantly knew I had to speak out for the sake of the people for whom the word was given.

I hesitated on going forth with the message, and instead spoke out, "the Holy Spirit is telling me that some of you in this room, in fact several, are depressed and in despair and do not want to continue in the calling you are in; that you are tired and weary and ready to throw in the towel this very day. If that describes you right now, come up right now and receive prayer, the Lord wants to refresh you and take that spirit of heaviness off you, and renew you for the battle ahead." The last word had no more than left my mouth, when the first of about six pastors jumped up and came forward for prayer. I was rather amazed at the response, but then thinking about the place we were in and what was just beyond the doors of the church, I realized that to have ten percent of these pastors ready to quit wasn't all that remarkable.

As I laid hands on them and began to pray for them, the mighty wind of the refreshing power of the Holy Spirit came upon them and knocked about four of the six off their feet. They fell back onto the dirty cement floor, laid there momentarily as the glory of the Lord settled in on them, and then they slowly began to get up and dust themselves off. God had done His mighty work! The pastors were invigorated and raised up for another day. As I went on to preach the message, I impressed upon them that Jesus, the Lord we serve, is a God of miracles, wonders, and signs, and that just when we think we have nothing left to give, God shows up to show us that though Him all things are possible, that what is impossible for man is nothing for God. Those precious pastors of Kibera, battling each day for souls that the enemy can so easily entrap in a place like that, have a very special place in the Lord's kingdom and their crowns in heaven will be abundant, and though their earthly reward may be insignificant, their main reward is yet to come.

For me to come into a place like that, from the prosperity and excess that we have here in the United States, and to encourage them not to give up in the race they have started, but to persevere to the finish line, was a very special mission. That is the reason why God sent me, and all of us, ten thousand miles on a mission. It was His plan, His timing, and He orchestrated all the events each and every day. As we were filing out at the end of the meeting, many of the pastors came up to shake my hand and were asking me, "Can you come back to Kibera for a series of meetings, for an outdoor crusade?" I answered without giving it much thought, "Yes, if it is the Lord's will, I will return."

CHAPTER 6

Kamiti Prison

Kamiti Maximum Security Prison is a very large prison about an hour outside of Nairobi. It was built to house fourteen hundred inmates, but now is home to over three thousand adult inmates, as well as several hundred youth offenders in a separate facility. The prison sits on a large parcel of land, over two thousand acres that are farmed by certain segments of the medium security prison population. Two brothers from the ministry team and me were taken out there by car early in the morning, so we could spend the day ministering to the inmates at the prison. It was an eye opening experience to say the least; Kamiti is the equivalent of Kibera slum in the prison world, it is a place of sodomy, brutality, and squalor and is included on some lists of the most violent prisons in the world.

I was used to going into prisons in the United States, I have been in several prisons and county jails to minister, but I definitely wasn't prepared for the squalor and cold starkness of Kamiti. By comparison, prisons in America look like the Hilton Hotel, for the most part the inmates in America are well fed and clothed, and have a fair amount of opportunities for vocational and counseling rehabilitation.

Not so in Kamiti, it was cramped and dirty. Upon arriving, we were taken to the warden's office for introductions, our team of three plus our female chaplain guide who would be our escort to the various venues throughout the day.

We entered the office of the warden to find a man who was very businesslike, yet compassionate in his desire to help the men in the prison attain to a better life as a result of their time incarcerated in the prison. After the introductions, the warden got straight to the point, even though he already knew what our purpose for coming was. "What is your purpose for being here?" He asked. As the spokesman for the group, I responded, "we are here in Nairobi with a large group of missionaries from America, and we wanted to come out and bless the men in Kamiti with a message of hope from the gospel." Then I went on to say, "I have a prison ministry back in Kansas in the USA, so God has put it on my heart to gather in the outcasts in prisons everywhere I go."

He looked pleased at the answer, and we could see the pride that he had in his job start to well up inside of him. "These are good men," he said, "Let's pray!" I was a bit taken back as we all held hands and stood in a circle and prayed for the message, the minister, and the men in the prison. No separation of church and state here, this man was bold in his faith and wasn't afraid to let the gospel message come forth wherever he was. It was quite refreshing to see after being in America where everyone is so timid and afraid they might offend someone or lose their job with a public display of their faith. We exited his office and from there headed out into the exercise or day yard to minister to a group of inmates.

The three of us, accompanied by our guide and an officer, entered the day yard, a dirt yard in the middle of the prison. We were taken to a picnic- type shelter in the middle of the yard that was the "stage" or center of focus for the session about to get underway. Then a group of men, maybe about one hundred or so, came out and started to mingle in the yard, and gathered with some who were already in the yard, sitting on the ground or lying in the sun on very thin foam mats. Their uniforms were black and white stripes, tattered and torn, very dirty; it looked as if some had not had a laundered uniform in quite some time. Three or four of the inmates came over to where we were and started to plug in instruments into a very crude sound system, and eventually it was up and running . A keyboard player, an electric guitar man, a drummer, a singer, along with lots of feedback and pops and crackles and soon everything was ready for the praise and worship to begin.

As we heard the band start to tune up and warm up, about thirty of the inmates formed three lines out in front of us and began to dance with the rhythm of the music, following the lead of a man who stood in front of them with his back to us. Their movements looked like a choreographed, rehearsed musical right out of Broadway in New York City! I had to pinch myself a time or two to make sure it was real, it was all so surreal; the movements all timed and in perfect unison, the black and white soiled zebra uniforms, the ten foot high walls of the prison with razor wire running on top all the way around, it was all just too much! My partners in ministry and I tried to jump in and dance with the inmates, and we kept up with them for about five minutes, and then we were finished. But the inmates kept going for about thirty minutes, all in perfect rhythm and movement, up and down, gyrating and spinning, hands and feet going in different directions.

As I watched in disbelief, I was struck by the fact that these men, in this most wretched and squalid of all places, had not only the joy of the Lord in their dance, but also their faces shined with joy. Their ear to ear smiles gave testimony as they danced that something inside of them had overcome their dismal and discouraging circumstances. It was certainly a blessing to me and my ministry mates, we who had come into the prison to bless the inmates, and we were the ones receiving the greatest blessings!

Eventually the inmates began to tire, and the dancing to the Lord session came to an end. Then my two brothers got up and each gave a brief testimony of what knowing the Lord Jesus had done in their life. I'm sure they were both greatly impacted by the service, as it was the first time for either of them to go into a prison anywhere.

What a way to start! I then got up and preached a message of hope to the inmates, a message of redemption and the power of Jesus to save and transform lives. I truly believe if these men could find joy in this place, under these circumstances, with many of them not going to be out of the prison for many years, then the joy of the Lord is truly available for every person in every walk of life!

As I gave an invitation at the end of the service for the men to come forward to make a confession of their faith in Jesus Christ, the only One who could truly forgive them of the sins and stumbling that had led them to this wretched place, many came forward with tears streaming down their cheeks, their heads bowed and their hands raised in the air. Many confessed Jesus, and many more came forward for prayers of healing and deliverance to cap off an utterly incredible service. This service will never be recorded on YouTube or even have one picture taken of it, but was certainly recorded in the books of heaven as one the Lord took special note. After praying for all the inmates and bidding them goodbye, we left that yard and prison and walked about a half mile to another section of the facility, this was the juvenile facility for young offenders under the age of eighteen.

The juvenile facility at Kamiti prison didn't carry the stench of despair and filth that was prevalent in the maximum adult facility; it was much cleaner and offered a ray of hope. Part of the reason for that was it was much smaller and closer to the fields and fresh air, on the edge of the prison building complex. In addition, the innocence of youth was evident in the faces and the smiles of the young men who were incarcerated there. We walked into a large room where about forty of them were waiting for us, and the joy of seeing the youth in there was a welcome contrast to where we had just been. As I surveyed the audience, I was touched by the sincere look on their faces, and the desire on the part of them to hear the encouraging words of the gospel, coming from a man from the United States who had come so far to come to visit them.

At the end of the message I preached, I asked those who wanted to accept Jesus as their Lord and Savior, or those who wanted to rededicate their life to Him, to come forward and make a public declaration of their faith. About a third of the young men in the room came forward, and as I prayed for them, the power of the Holy Spirit came in like a refreshing wind and touched each one with a mighty touch. The tears flowed down, and true repentance and sorrow came gushing out in a range of emotion and physical manifestation. Hands were up in the air, some were on their knees, some crying, some rejoicing with great smiles of joy on their faces, and the reactions ran the gamut of human emotion.

And through it all, the Holy Spirit was molding hearts and minds to be obedient to Him, so that when these young people would someday get out of prison, they would have a decent chance of living a respectable, law abiding life, not having to fall back on lying and stealing to make it through to the next day. As we wrapped up our day of ministry at Kamiti, it was with great joy and satisfaction in knowing we had done our best in bringing hope and the good news of the gospel to the outcasts of that very depressing place; and in knowing that God was with these precious souls in Kamiti. We left nodding in agreement with the warden's description, "These are good men!"

CHAPTER 7
All Church Picnic

All the preaching and evangelism events of the week were intended to stir interest in the final evangelism push, the All Church Picnic, to be held at Uhuru Park in central Nairobi on Saturday at the end of the week. I had the privilege to preach at several churches and the Kamiti prison, so I, along with everyone on the mission team was eagerly anticipating the grand finale. One of the churches that I spoke in during the week was the All Nations Gospel Church near Kibera, a church that was dedicated in 1968 during an Oral Roberts Crusade in Nairobi. I was told before speaking there, that famed evangelists Oral Roberts himself, and another famous American evangelist T. L. Osborne, had both stood in the very pulpit that I was standing in before the noonday crowd that was gathered that day. And so it was a humbling, and at the same time exhilarating experience to walk in the footsteps of some of the great American evangelists who had visited Nairobi many years before.

As our team descended upon Uhuru Park on Friday, the day before the main event, we were reminded of the scripture in Hebrews, "*therefore we also, since we are surrounded by so great a cloud of witnesses, let us lay aside every weight, and the sin which so easily ensnares us, and let us run with endurance the race that is set before us."* (Hebrews 12:1) Uhuru Park is that place in Nairobi where a person certainly feels the presence of the great cloud of witnesses, as it has played host to scores of western evangelists who have visited

Africa over the years, and it is a place that could easily be described as designed for preaching large crusades. The park itself is about thirty acres that sits adjacent to the Nairobi business and financial district, and is a welcome break in the filth and noise of the typical Nairobi day. But the crowning feature of the park is a natural amphitheater bowl that descends down to a large plaza at the base of the hill. The grass covered hillside will easily accommodate one hundred thousand people or more, and some crusades have claimed as many as two hundred thousand have come in a single service to hear the gospel being preached. So it was with much anticipation that we prayer walked through the park and over the grounds that Friday, praying for people to come, and for the Holy Spirit to touch those in attendance with power for salvation and healing.

When Saturday rolled around, we were up and out to the grounds by midmorning, with the service scheduled to begin about noon with choirs and musicians from several local churches leading the way, followed by our own mission team worship band, and then the gospel message. As the service began to unfold, we could see the crowd was going to be small, especially in comparison to the level of expectation. But the people who were there were enjoying the worship music and the choirs, and then they settled into a time of listening to brother Daniel, as he brought a dramatic presentation to life, depicting the questions and thoughts going through the mind of the man who made the cross upon which Jesus was crucified. This presentation prepared the audience for the final message, a message of hope and healing from brother Stephen. It ended with an altar call, and invitation for those who wished to make a decision about accepting Jesus as their Lord to come down to the plaza at the bottom of the hill. Several of the pastors and ministers, along with me, stood at the base of the hill to receive those who came down, to pray with them for salvation and to receive the Holy Spirit and also to receive healing.

I was standing next to a Kenyan pastor who could speak Swahili to anyone who came down, and we spoke to many about their desire to receive Jesus. Then toward the end of the time of the altar call, a lady came down and stood before me. She looked as if she had been through a lot; her hair was a bit disheveled, she looked like she had a lot of pain for her young age, the trials and torment crying out from the pain in her eyes and on her face. In her hands she held a small child, and she came and stood right in front of me and the pastor, and as he spoke to her in Swahili, the image of the lady in a vision given to the prison inmate back in Kansas came swirling into my head. Then the Holy Spirit spoke to me, "This is her, the one given to the inmate in a vision."

As the pastor continued to speak to her, I asked her if I could pray for her. She nodded yes, and indicated she had come to confess Jesus as her Lord and Savior. So I prayed for her to receive Jesus, and for Him to refresh and renew her from the difficult life and the trials of which she had. With tears streaming down her cheeks, she received the prayers for her salvation and for healing. And then when we got to the end of our conversation, I asked her, "What is the name of your child?" She said to us, "His name is Immanuel."

I took a step back and gazed in awe at the two of them, and the way the Holy Spirit had orchestrated the events of the day. I was in awe that the one seen in the inmate's vision was standing in front of me, but also that of all names the child could have, his name was Immanuel, which means "God with us." My heart leapt as I thought about my brother back in the prison who was going to be praying for this child all the rest of his life, that every time this child was brought to his mind, he would be reminded that God is with us. And so the day ended on that beautiful high note, a reminder that God knows the beginning from the end and middle of all things, even things yet to come.

When I got back to Kansas, I went into the prison on Friday night as I always did, and I told the brother who had the vision about the lady, that she had come down to stand in front of me at the Uhuru Park crusade. And then I told him about her child, and that the child's name was Immanuel, and that he would be praying for Immanuel all the rest of the days of his life. When I spoke the word Immanuel, he just stepped back and started to cry, he had no words for what God had done, just tears. The Lord works in mysterious ways!

CHAPTER 8

Maasai Mara

The spiritual warfare encountered by the team during the week of preaching and worship was intense, as any time you take on the enemy in his territory he will defend and attack to maintain his turf. The unseen battles in a place like Africa, where there is so much witchcraft and other demonic oppression, leaves a person a bit exhausted and ready for a bit of relaxation. What a better way to do that than to go to the Maasai Mara, the giant game preserve in southern Kenya, home to many of the world's most beautiful wild animals. The Maasai Mara is a park of over five hundred fifty square miles in size, and is famous around the globe for its populations of lions, cheetahs, leopards, elephants, rhinos, hippos, and many other migrating animals such as the zebra and wildebeest. Our team had fanned out on Sunday to minister in several churches across Nairobi, and then we came back together Sunday evening to rest up for the trip to the Mara.

We were all up bright and early on Monday morning, waiting for the guides from the safari company to come pick us up for the three hour trip to the Maasai Mara. Three Land Rovers came rolling in at eight in the morning, and we all piled in, anxiously anticipating the three days of relaxation that we knew we were going to enjoy, taking in the sights of the beauty of some of God's finest creation. As we came rolling into our lodging headquarters at the Mara around noon, we were amazed at what would be our temporary home for the next two nights and three days. We were going to be lodging in tents right out on the preserve; our hosts were owners from America of a tent complex, that from the outside looked like basic army tents, but inside were very elegant and beautifully adorned.

Each tent was to be occupied by either a married couple, or two or three single people, and guarded at night by a Maasai warrior who stood at guard at the front of the tent. Because the safari lodge was on the Mara and therefore the wild animals could come right up to the tents, it was a necessity to have a warrior with a spear and knife at the entrance. Stories drifted around over the three days about elephants who had come up to the tents to "rearrange the deck furniture," and we could hear leopards screaming out in the night. All the electricity used was off grid and provided by solar or wind powered generators, and the food and service was nothing short of fabulous, especially considering we were so far off the beaten path, in Kenya no less.

The daily routine was certainly conducive to relaxation and great fun, with photography quickly becoming the number one activity for all the members of the team. We were up early each day, ready for a great breakfast of tea, rolls, and omelets, then we would pile into the Land Rovers and head out onto the Mara to look for the "big five," the lions, cheetahs, leopard, rhinos, and hippos. While looking for those, we often went by huge herds of wildebeest, zebras, African buffalo, impalas, and many other animals of every size and description. Lesser numbers of other animals seen included élans, giraffes, antelopes, and gazelles, and we even passed a few hyena and ostrich. Truly a menagerie of God's creation, and to see them in their native habitat was absolutely awe inspiring.

The second day out we were stopped on a road not far from a pride of lions, and one female lion came walking across within five feet of the front of our Land Rover. She had a big chunk of a wildebeest or some other animal in her mouth; it was still fresh and dripping with blood as she seemed oblivious to our presence. We were all quiet except for the sound of the camera shutters going off, and she nonchalantly went on about her business as if we weren't even there.

The guides told us, "As long as you stay in the Land Rover you will be were completely safe, as the animals have grown used to the landscape with vehicles moving about." But he also said," if you get out of the vehicle and attempt to walk across the Mara, you will quickly be dead meat, either to a pride of lions, or to the universally feared African buffalo." They are considered by most of the guides to be the most aggressive of all the animals on the Mara, and they would quickly spot a human and take them out. While cruising along the Maasai River that afternoon, we were privileged to see an old hippopotamus slowly meandering off into the bush away from the river. Our guide explained to us, "She is probably going out into the bush to die. She won't last long in the condition she is in, the lions or hyenas will make short work of her out there so far from the river."

At night back at the safari lodge, after supper we would gather around a campfire out in the back yard of the camp. As the blackness of the Kenyan sky gradually enveloped us, the fire became a very welcome attraction, not only for light and safety from the wild animals, but also for the warmth it provided to counter the chill of the evening. One night while sitting around the campfire reminiscing about the events and scenes of the day, we were taken by total surprise by about twenty Maasai warriors who came out of the darkness and surrounded our group around the campfire. They proceeded to grab some of the ladies in the group and incorporate them into a native Maasai dance, we assumed to be a courtship dance of some type that never was explained, but I'm sure the ladies were quite happy it was all just in fun!

Then another dance to the beat of a single drum ensued where all the warriors jumped up in the air on cue. Talk about vertical leap, they could have all had basketball scholarships to any college in America. Some of us men got up and joined their "jump dance," but were unsuccessful at rising up over a foot above the ground. And so it was a fun night around the campfire. We drank hot tea, and watched the Maasai in their bright colored native clothing, dancing the dances that spoke of centuries and millennia of their culture, herding animals and protecting their livestock and families from the wild animals. It was quite a memorable adventure to say the least.

On the third morning we began to pack up our bags, since the plan was to drive out across the Maasai Mara and then head back to Nairobi about noon, to be back to the city before nightfall. As we gathered around the breakfast lodge, we shed tears thinking about having to leave our gracious hosts and this most beautiful of God's creations. We gathered as a group and took many pictures of the mission team with the Maasai hosts, and then of different individuals in various groups. The final goodbye was held up as brother Daniel stepped forward and gave a short salvation message and invitation to our hosts. Daniel was always looking for ways to bring more souls into the kingdom of God. He never got so relaxed he forgot why we were in Africa, and he gently laid out the gospel plan of salvation and then invited any who wanted to step forward and make a decision. None came forward, as many of the Maasai are already believers in Jesus Christ as their Lord, and that was apparently the case with these at this camp. But it was a memorable time, and we said goodbye to the Maasai Mara with a tear in our eye as we headed back to Nairobi, and two days later back to America.

CHAPTER 9

Kibera Crusade 2011

The words that I had spoken to the Kibera pastors on the way out the door, that "if it is the Lord's will, I will return," became prophetic words the next year as I received an invitation from the pastors to return to Kibera for an outdoor crusade. I had done a Daniel fast and prayer throughout the month of January, and the Holy Spirit just continued to speak to me, "Kibera, Kibera." So I contacted Pastor Jacob in Nairobi to see what he thought about the idea, and he was very enthusiastic about it. "I will get in touch with the Kibera pastors and we will see about when the best time would be to have it, when the weather would be good and no chance for rain," he said. And then he asked, "How many days would you like to go, and what would you like to call it?" After a bit of thought, I boldly declared, "Let's go for five nights outdoors, and we'll call it the Kibera Catch the Fire Miracle Crusade!" Nothing timid about that name, or setting up in the middle of Kibera for five days, we were going to go for a big harvest.

I had never been into the heart of the Kibera slum, just driven around the outside edges of it on the paved roads, so I was a bit unsure of what the logistics would be of setting up right in the heart of Kibera. But I knew I had a burning desire to bring souls to the Lord, and God was opening a big door of opportunity for me there. I have learned over the years when God opens up a door of opportunity, it is best if at all possible to go through it, not only for kingdom sake, but also for the sake of my fulfillment and joy. So I let Pastor Jacob know we were going to go for it; that he and Pastor Michael were to organize the other pastors and I would begin immediately raising money to pay for all the necessities for an outdoor crusade of this type. We would have to contract sound system technicians and sound services, praise and worship bands, platform erection, security, and advertising such as thousands of posters and banners to hang across the roads leading into Kibera.

It was a big undertaking and required lots of planning and coordination. We were planning to start on Wednesday and go through Sunday night, with the platform setup to be on Tuesday. Each day's program would be three hours of praise and worship led by three different worship bands, followed by an hour of preaching and then an altar call, after which I would be ushered into a car and taken out of Kibera no later than eight o'clock each night.

The crusade was to be held in the Kamukunji grounds, an open space of a few acres right in the heart of the Kibera slum. Kamukunji grounds have a history and legend all its own; it has been the gathering place for many political meetings over the years, as well as the sight for the Oral Roberts Crusade in 1968. It is surrounded on all sides by tin shacks about eight feet square, and small business and retail stores also housed in tin shacks about the same size. Open ditches of sewage and waste water flow down a couple sides of the grounds, and on a third side is a dust buried railroad track, the pathway for the daily commuter train that goes from downtown Nairobi to the far east side of the city and back a few times each day.

The first day of the crusade I was standing on the platform preaching, it was about six-thirty in the evening and the daily commuter was barreling out from downtown and came right through our crusade crowd. I was taken by complete surprise by it, and thought sure some of the crowd was going to get wiped out by the train, but by the grace of God, everyone jumped away from the tracks just in time to keep from getting wiped out!

The entry into the grounds was down a dirt road, severely rutted out from rain and lack of any attention or repair, winding through the never ending sea of humanity and eight foot square shacks. On each side of the car there was just enough room for a person carrying a heavy load on their back or on a bicycle, to make their way in and out of Kamukunji up to the main road that circled Kibera. Twice each day I traversed that road for five days, once in the light of the afternoon and once in the dark of night. Needless to say, it was a new experience for an evangelist from Kansas to be in the heart of this rough place, where I so easily stood out and could have been an easy target, but the Lord was good to me and protected me and my drivers every step of the way.

When our church team went to Kamukunji on Tuesday to set up the platform and make preparations for the crusade, they were met by homeless squatters who called Kamukunji their home. They felt like our team was encroaching on their territory. In a sense they were right, but our team had a permit in hand that said we had the rights to the grounds from three until eight at night, from Tuesday until Sunday, and so because of that our team was intent on setting up and removing them. When the squatters became belligerent, the police were called in to remove them, but in the ensuing scuffle, some of the squatters attacked the police with machetes, and two of the attackers were shot and killed.

So that is the way the Kibera crusade started, in an intense spiritual warfare battle that was playing out in the heavenlies, but manifesting in battles in the earthly realm over the grounds. I was not part of the setup crew, so I was not aware that all this was happening; the pastors made a point to not inform me, they wanted to shield me from any bad news, fear, or intimidation, as they themselves did not know what was going to happen during the crusade. The possibility existed that the attackers would be back and try to disrupt or in some way try to stop the crusade. I didn't find out until Sunday that all this had taken place on setup day, and because the squatters came back to disrupt on Sunday, I was told the whole story about their complaint and actions.

When Wednesday rolled around, I was taken by car to the grounds about three in the afternoon, and enjoyed the praise and worship for several hours by three different bands, the Judah Band from Nairobi, the JC Band from Congo, and Naomi from Tassia. They were awesome in getting the crowd going and bringing us into the presence of the Lord. The African people love to dance, rhythm is in their DNA and anytime there is praise music going on, they are drawn to it and will stay and dance to the Lord as long as the music is going. The challenge in Kibera, according to the pastors there, is to get the people to stay around to listen to the preacher after the music is over.

The first night I went out onto the platform, I had my Bible in my right hand, and a big white feed bag in my left hand that was about a third full of big ear corn; on the front of the bag were the words "Revelation 22," just as I had seen in the dream the Lord had given me a couple of years earlier. I knew this was the fulfillment of the prophetic dream He had given me that I was standing on the very platform I had been standing on in the dream.

I was preaching in English, and the pastor beside me was translating into Swahili, and I told the people at the outset that I was here to bring them a word that had been declared to me in a prophetic dream. I was not there by accident or just by my good idea, but God had appointed me to come and bring the good news of Revelation 22 to them for a time such as this, that this was the appointed time.

After that introduction, I began to preach the message of "Jesus, the Living Water," and the people stayed around to listen. I prayed also for the people to catch the fire, as this was the name of the crusade and in a very real way, the Lord wanted the poor people of Kibera to catch the fire of the Holy Spirit. It was an exciting and incredible night! At the altar call it was dark and many began to stream forward either to make a decision to accept Jesus as their Lord and Savior, or to receive prayers for healing. In African crusades there are always two calls to the altar; one for confession of faith, another for healing.

Many times the children come rushing forward for the first call, and it is humorously said in Africa that most of the children have been saved many times. They have the innocence to come rushing forward, while the adults with the pride and the bondages stand and mull over their decisions, and sometimes never do get around to making one. At the altar call that first night, we had over one hundred people come forward to make a salvation decision, and many more than that come forward for prayers for healing. Those who made a decision about salvation were ushered off to one side, so the pastors could get their name and phone number, which is the only way to trace most people in Kibera, as there are no addresses or other ways to track them.

The altar call itself lasted about an hour, and by the time I prayed for those receiving Jesus, and then laying hands on the many that had come forward for prayers for healing, I was exhausted and at the same time exhilarated at the response. All I could think as I was getting into the car was, "Thank you, Lord, for your goodness and mercy, to allow Your servant the opportunity to come here to the meek and the poor and preach the good news of the gospel." About that time one of the pastors accompanying me to the car said to me, "Jim, you have favor to preach here in Kibera, the people stayed around after the music to hear the word!" So they were excited as well.

On the way home the driver told me that when I was praying for the people to "catch the fire," the Lord had opened his spiritual eyes and he had seen fire coming down from heaven and touching every one of the people on the head, just as on the day of Pentecost, in the book of Acts, chapter two. As we made our way up the rough and dusty road worming its way out of Kamukunji, all I could say was "Yes, Lord!"

After the first four nights of the crusade we were all beginning to get a bit tired, but we were seeing great response from the outcasts of Kibera. After the first four services more than six hundred people had come forward to accept Jesus Christ as their Lord and Savior, and hundreds more had come forward to receive prayers for healing.

There had also been a lot of spiritual warfare along the way, the main one battling the sound system that was old and a bit underpowered to carry the sound above the noise of Kibera. Many of the shops in Kibera have their own little sound systems blaring to attract attention to their place, and there are quite a few small motorcycles in the area as well, so the background noise is something that has to be reckoned with.

But after a few replacement parts were inserted into speakers, more powerful amps, and some better microphones, about half way through the second night's service, the sound started to gel and get much better. All of that is pretty typical for Africa, you just have to roll with the punches and be patient, few things work over there exactly like they are supposed to, or like they do here in America. In America, we are used to everything going off like clockwork, on time and with all the bells and whistles running, but in Africa it seldom happens that way.

When Sunday, the final day of the crusade came along, we were all looking forward to the grand finale, and we were in expectation that the Lord was going to do something mighty on the final day. After going to church that morning, a group of us were headed over after church to Kibera, and we planned to stop along the way and have some good Kenyan chicken at a fast food restaurant. Pastor Jacob, three ladies from the church who were going to the crusade, and myself stopped to eat and had just sat down to eat our chicken and chips when the Pastor received a call from another of the pastors who was already down at the crusade grounds in Kamukunji.

He said to Pastor Jacob, "You keep Jim there eating chicken for a while, the squatters are back and they have taken over the crusade grounds. They have their own little sound system up on the stage, and they are holding a funeral service for the two of their brothers who were shot and killed by the police last Tuesday! We will call you back when it is safe to bring Jim down here, till then just stay at the chicken shack."

As Pastor Jacob was relaying all this to me, I am thinking, "Huh? What? What are you talking about? Where is our security team?" I had not been told until now about the killings on the day of the setup, for fear I might run the other way and not show up for the crusade. So the warfare battle was just starting to intensify, the devil was pulling out all the stops to try to keep us from finishing the crusade on a high note.

As it turned out, our security team that I had sent money on ahead to Kenya to contract, was nowhere to be seen when the squatters came around about noon to have the funeral, they had all gone to church on Sunday morning! So the squatters just helped themselves to the stage, put their sound system up on it, and were determined they were going to have a funeral in the Kamukunji grounds, no matter what. No amount of talking by the pastors could persuade them that they needed to give up and peacefully move aside so we could start at the appointed time. So as the three o'clock start time came and went, we were still at the chicken shack, getting real impatient and quite tired of nibbling on chicken bones.

Finally, about four o'clock, a call came from Pastor Michael in Kibera that it was all clear, and it was time to bring me down so we could commence with the last day of the crusade. We finally got things started about four-thirty, an hour and a half later than planned, but in Africa everything is always "Hakuna Matata," or no worries as they say. We also contacted the local police and asked for an extension on the permitted time for the end of the crusade, and they willingly granted us to stay until nine that night, so we were happy about that as well. As the praise and worship bands began to play and a crowd began to gather, all was good and I was again thanking the Lord for His grace and mercy, as no one got hurt and we were able to amicably settle the argument and proceed with the crusade.

As I was standing behind the platform praying, waiting to go up onto the platform to begin to preach the message for the final time, I was struck by the utter hopelessness of the setting of Kibera, compared to the wealth of the place I come from in America. Here I was standing beside an open ditch of sewage running behind the platform, preaching in a place where disease and sickness are rampant; where most of the people call a rusted out tin shack of less than one hundred square feet their home, and survive on less than a dollar a day. The contrast was magnified when after this crusade, and another in west Kenya, I would be hopping on an airplane and flying back to America, to a land where most people have all the material blessings, including hospitals and doctors, that any person on this earth could ever hope for.

The contrast was overwhelming, but it gave me even more incentive to go out that last night and preach my heart out; that Jesus is the only hope that does not disappoint; that truly He is the Father to the fatherless, the One who truly cares for the widow, the orphan, and the outcasts of the world, including those in Kibera.

That final night all the Kibera pastors came forward to stand on the platform and receive recognition, and then I was given the platform to bring one more message to the people of Kibera. I preached about Jesus our Healer, the One who shed His blood not only for our salvation, but also for our healing. Of the hundreds who had come forward for prayers for healing during the week, some had been given miraculous healings and had come up onto the platform to give testimonies, so it was a fitting way to end the week of crusade meetings, proclaiming the good news of Jesus as our Eternal Healer.

At the end of the message, I gave an altar call one more time, and again over one hundred people came forward to confess their faith in Jesus as Lord, and another several hundred came forward to ask for prayers for healing. It was a dramatic end to the week, where altogether over seven hundred people gave their life to Jesus and many more were healed. After climbing in the car and winding one last time up and out of Kamukunji, I had given my all; and not only that, I was forever changed, as well as many of the people in Kibera. I was about to explode with the emotion along with the fire of the Holy Spirit. It was a very moving experience for me, and as we were driving home that night, I wanted to cry and shout for joy all at the same time; cry for the utter hopelessness of the poverty of Kibera, but joy for those who had put their hope in Jesus Christ! Jesus said it best, "Blessed are the poor in spirit, for theirs is the kingdom of heaven."

CHAPTER 10
Mumias Crusade 2011

After the week in Kibera, we all rested up a couple of days and then took off for Mumias, a city of about twenty thousand people out in west Kenya, about six hours by car west of Nairobi, and only about an hour from the Uganda border. Mumias is in a lush area of Kenya, not far from the equator where rainfall is abundant and food is plentiful, unlike some other areas of Kenya and Africa. The farmers' markets and roadside stands are full of the whole spectrum of fruits and vegetables, everything from avocados and pineapples, to sweet potatoes, tomatoes, and greens.

Mumias is also home to the Mumias Sugar Company, the largest sugar producer in Kenya, which it makes from crushed sugar cane, and so it is a busy place with many tractors and huge wagons of sugar cane going back and forth to the plant from the cane fields in the surrounding countryside. The tractors and wagons constantly clog up the roads and highways in every direction away from the city, and for the pedestrian or those on bicycles, it is a very dangerous place to travel. Of the times I have been to Mumias, it always seems to be harvest time, and the people who work in the sugar plant and the related farms, appear to always be in a hurry.

The Lord linked me in 2010 with Pastor Luke from Mumias, and he had invited me to come out and preach a crusade, and at the same time we would hold a pastor training and encouragement for local pastors in the west Kenya, eastern Uganda area. The planned program was to hold the pastor training at Pastor Luke's church from nine until noon each day, then break a couple hours for lunch, then go to the crusade ground at the junction of two highways about a half mile away from the church from three until six in the evening.

And if that wasn't enough, then go back to the church and hold revival from seven until nine at night, and do that for four days. Talk about an intense schedule! My part was to get up on the platform and preach the crusade, while other area pastors would share the responsibility of preaching at the pastor training and the revival. We also had some very good praise and worship leaders and bands at this crusade, and each day we started at three o'clock with some local church worship bands and choirs.

Before the week had ended, over two hundred people had come forward to accept Jesus as their Lord, and again many more had come forward for healing and deliverance. Many who came forward were out of the Muslim faith, as there are many Muslims in the region. When we had a baptism service in a local river at the end of the week, many of the teenagers who came down into the water to be baptized were former Muslims, and I asked Pastor Luke to identify those to me that he knew to be out of that faith. It was a wonderful sight to see so many young people who received the truth of the gospel, even if it meant being shunned and turned out of their family home. For some in Africa, to make a commitment to Jesus is a very costly decision, it can cost them everything, including their families and all their possessions.

Pastor Luke's father himself had been a Muslim but had been converted to Christianity at age fifty, and there were many children in the family, some Muslim and some raised Christian. One of the brothers of Luke had been a Muslim and had a son named David, and because the HIV virus had gone through their community and family with a vengeance, it left all the wives of the brother of Luke dead, and the brother himself had contracted AIDS, as well as David had contracted AIDS. When I preached that first day on the platform at Mumias, I saw David in the audience; he looked very weak and pale, he was certainly sick and was in the death throes of AIDS. At the altar call he was the first one to come forward to receive Jesus as Lord, and after praying for him for salvation, I also prayed for him to be healed of AIDS. He was so weak he could barely stand up under the weight of the glory of the Lord, some of the people standing next to him had to hold him up to receive the prayers. And later that week at the baptism service, he was the first to go down into the water to be baptized, he was zealous for the Lord to heal him, and he came with the anticipation and innocence of the child of twelve years that he was.

But God did not disappoint David; I saw him the next year when I went back to Mumias to preach another crusade, and he looked like a totally different person. He had a sparkle in his eye and his step was lively, and he was able to do some work on the farm where he lived, helping out with the chores and the vegetable gardening. I have been able to keep in touch with David since then, and he is still doing well; he is in school and moving on with his life. I believe the Lord gave him a miraculous healing from AIDS; it certainly appears that he has been given new life. "Bwana Asifiwe!" Or as they say in Swahili, Praise the Lord!

The baptism service at the end of the week was a glorious affair, held in a local river about a mile outside of Mumias. We arose early that morning and headed for the church, and about nine in the morning we all started to walk towards the river. It looked like a parade of several pastors, church members, and those who were to be baptized along with their families. It was a bright and sunny day, fitting for the occasion; the haze of the morning had burned off, leaving nothing but the deep blue sky, and the hustle and bustle of another day in Africa. When we got to the river, four of us pastors got down into the waist deep water, which was a bit chilly but soon we became accustomed to it.

As the families and those to be baptized gathered on the bank of the river, spontaneous singing began to break out, and the melodies continued throughout the time of the service. The music drifted up over the dancing noise of the small waterfall, which was cascading over the rocks under a bridge a short distance away. One by one the babes in Christ waded into the water, many of them teenagers, many from Muslim families who were stepping out in faith into a whole new territory of commitment. The songs of the families, the dancing music of the water, the prayers of the pastors over those being immersed, and the joy of the Lord present in all those who were there, all contributed to a surreal feeling as if to say, "It doesn't get any better than this here on this earth."

Altogether we baptized about forty people, and as they came up out of the water, a pastor was there with a towel to wipe the water from their face and to shout over them, "Bwana Asifiwe!" It was truly a glorious time, a time for which a pastor or minister of the gospel yearns for. Later that day I was to travel by car to Kisumu, a two hour ride south of Mumias, where I would get on a plane and head back to Nairobi, so I cherished the memory of that joyous time at the river in my heart as I got on the plane at Kisumu.

CHAPTER 11

Goma,

Democratic Republic of Congo

In the spring of 2012 I received a call from Pastor Jacob in Nairobi, he was excitedly telling me about an opportunity, an open door to go into the Democratic Republic of Congo that coming summer to conduct crusade and pastor training. The city we would be going to was Goma, a city of a million people on the east side of the Congo, a city I later found out was the epicenter of rebel warfare that had been going on in that part of the Congo for about thirty years.

Goma is the capitol of North Kivu State, a large state that joins Rwanda and Uganda to the east, and is a very rich area of Congo in terms of natural resources; timber products, but more importantly diamonds, gold, tungsten, and coltan, a precious metal used in computer touch screen manufacturing. All are found in abundance in North Kivu, and so it became a battleground for those rebel groups, some from neighboring countries, some from disgruntled Congolese army troops, who came into North Kivu and set up territory to extract out the minerals and send them out of the country for sale.

But in addition to establishing areas of rebel control, along with that came the terrorizing of local villagers and farmers who were caught in the middle of the ongoing warfare. The rebels on one side, and the government and United Nations peacekeepers and troops who were trying to rid the land of the rebels on the other, and keep a semblance of peace established. Along with the rebel groups came kidnapping of teenagers who were of use to the rebels to carry weapons and fight for them, and many rapes of women, young and old, who were caught in the crossfire.

East Congo and North Kivu have earned the reputation over the years of the conflict as the "rape capitol of the world," and the ongoing turmoil had left many women scarred with great emotional wounds, not to mention the pain inflicted by the general instability and insecurity of the whole region. And so it was into this setting that the Lord was asking us to go, to bring the hope of the gospel and encouragement to the brothers and sisters of the church in Goma and the surrounding area, an area that certainly needed encouragement if there ever was a place.

Pastor Jacob had met another young pastor in Nairobi, a Pastor Isaiah, a Congolese refugee who, along with his wife and children, had fled the rebel warfare in Congo and had sought refuge in the stability of Kenya. He, along with another Congolese refugee living in Nairobi, brother Mark, were our links into the pastors' association that would be hosting the crusade and meetings in Goma. We also were planning to meet with the government officials in Goma, as it is the capitol city of North Kivu, and in addition, brother Mark's cousin was the Governor of North Kivu State, so we had a personal connection to the Governor.

As the plans were being laid out, it was all very exciting to think the Lord was going to use us in this way to help bring peace and stability into the region of Goma. One of the lessons of spiritual warfare is this: if there is great chaos and turmoil going on in the natural world, in the politics and events in the daily existence of the people there, then in the spirit world you also know there is a great battle going on, as the devil always wants to create chaos, mayhem, death and destruction wherever he can. And so a team of five of us was planning to make the trip; Pastor Jacob, his wife Anna, Pastor Isaiah, brother Mark, and myself.

I arrived in Nairobi in late August to meet up with the team and begin the mission, only to find out that we had not been able to obtain our visas to enter into the Congo. It seems that the Congolese government was not issuing visas at this time, the rebel activity was very intense around the Goma area. There was actually a rebel army of a couple thousand men perched just a few kilometers outside of Goma, with a refugee camp of displaced villagers of several hundred thousand people sandwiched between the rebels and the city of Goma. They had been forced to flee from their homes and villages in the area north of Goma, next to the neighboring country of Uganda, where many of the rebels came from.

Without the visas in hand we were stuck in Nairobi, no visa no entry, so it was a particularly urgent situation because we had already sent ahead to the pastors in Goma several thousands of dollars for the preparations for the crusades and meetings. Posters and banners advertising the meeting, sound systems, hall rental, hotel room rental, musicians and praise bands, all that had already been contracted and paid for, so as we sat in Nairobi with no visas, it became a very frustrating and distressful situation.

Pastor Jacob and I made a visit to the Congolese Embassy in Nairobi, where we had an appointment with an official of the embassy to discuss the visa situation, but we left there with no promises as the information coming to him from the Congolese government basically said this: "No visas issued to missionaries at this time, it is just too dangerous around Goma, and we don't want to be responsible for them." So as we mulled our chances to go, the time to depart was rapidly approaching with still no visas in hand.

We prayed about strategy to get the visas, and a light went on in Mark's head, and he exclaimed, "I'll contact my cousin, the Governor, and he will get us our visas!" We all thought "hmm, that must be the reason brother Mark is with us, as he had no other outlined duties of ministry on the upcoming trip, but he had been placed with us to help part the way where there was no way." Sure enough, after a series of phone calls to the Governor and his staff, red tape was starting to be cut, and three days later, just a day before the scheduled date of departure, we went back to the Congolese Embassy to pick up our visas. God is good, as they say, and that was just one of many small miracles that were to ensue on the trip into the Congo.

The next day the five of us got on the plane in Nairobi headed for Kigali, Rwanda, and from there we would rent a car to travel the four hour trip through western Rwanda, to Goma in the Congo. There were no direct plane flights into Goma except military and United Nations planes because of the rebel activity, but the flight into Kigali was smooth and uneventful as we completed the first leg of the journey.

Kigali, the capitol city of Rwanda, is a beautiful city of over a million people, located in the geographic center of Rwanda. Kigali is built on several hills, with bustling business, financial, and government centers on each of the tops of the ridges, and housing and apartments located more in the valleys and low lying areas. The most striking thing about Kigali, and all of Rwanda, is how spotlessly clean it is compared to Kenya and other places in Africa I had been. Not one single plastic bag, cup, or stray piece of paper was seen anywhere in the city, even the vacant lots were clean and all the streets and sidewalks downtown were spotless.

It was told to me that even the President of the country gets out and helps pick up trash on the monthly cleanup days, but at this point I wouldn't think he would find a whole lot to do. Couple the cleanliness of the country with the tropical lush vegetation, the beautiful flowers and trees, and the tidy, manicured farms and tea plantations, and truly it appears to be a tropical paradise. Rwanda reminded me in many ways of Costa Rica, a country I had come to know through several mission trips from 2006-2009, when I went into some of the most wild and pristine land in all of Costa Rica.

We arrived uneventfully in Kigali, and then rented a car for the four hour trip to Goma, a trip that would take us through western Rwanda, an area of mountains, some very high and others more like hills and ridges, with the slopes of the smaller mountains neatly terraced for farming, and all the valleys and areas around the villages cultivated to the last square foot of available space. Many of the valleys contained tea farms, and I learned that Rwandan tea is actually quite famous in eastern Africa. Besides tea, the whole gamut of vegetable and fruit crops were grown; fields of sweet potatoes, different strains of regular potatoes, many varieties of greens, tomatoes, squash, and acre after acre of pole beans, and field corn, the staple of all African countries. The farms throughout western Rwanda were just as neat and manicured as the city of Kigali, it was a beautiful sight to see after so many of the slums, trash, and squalor of Kenya.

After winding our way through the mountainous terrain, we started to descend into the area of Goma, first passing through the last city we would go through in Rwanda, the city of Gisenyi, and then cross over the border into the Goma. As we approached the sign over the border which read "Welcome to the Democratic Republic of Congo," my spirit leapt as I knew something great was in store for us and for the kingdom, for all the trouble and sacrifice it had taken to get this far.

Immediately after proudly displaying our visas and passing through the border checkpoint, we were met by a contingent of Goma pastors, the ones who would be hosting the meetings. We learned a few things from them that would alter the course of our plans; that there would be no outdoor crusade because of the heightened security issues, and that we had rented a hall in the city center that was behind a ten foot high wall with razor wire on the top. The pastor training would be held from nine until noon each day, and then we would break for lunch and be back for the indoor crusade at three in the afternoon, and then would be required to exit the building by six in the evening to be back at our hotel before dark. That would be the program for the next three days, with the final night of the crusade to be Sunday night. We planned to meet with the Governor and his staff on Monday, and then fly back to Nairobi from Gisenyi on Tuesday of the following week.

The sights and sounds of Goma were peculiar and a bit intimidating to say the least. The spiritual warfare going on around the city, due to the rebel activity and the overwhelming troop presence, was quite pronounced. At least ten thousand United Nations troops and a few thousand Congolese troops were present in the city to guard against the rebel aim to take over Goma. Every street was filled with armored troop carriers, Humvees, and trucks carrying supplies to the refugees and the troops who were guarding the city. A spirit of fear and despair had crept in over the city, and it was a time for people to hunker down and just pray that God would protect them and their city.

The physical presence of the city of Goma is a bit discouraging as well. Just a few kilometers north of the city, a huge volcanic mountain, Mt. Nyiragongo, juts up into the horizon, a now flattop mountain because of the eruption in 2002 that forced two hundred thousand people of Goma to evacuate their homes. The lava flow, which in some places was several feet deep, burned many homes and businesses, and eventually claimed one hundred and fifty lives. The mountain hovers over the city and still spews smoke constantly, as if to remind all the residents of Goma that they are really just temporary residents of the city, that the mountain is the reminder that God is really the one who has the final say so of who stays, and for how long.

Another peculiar characteristic of the city is that because of the lava flow throughout the city, which in some places was six feet deep and a thousand yards wide, all the streets, except for a few main throughfares which are paved, are of lava rock that solidified after the lava flow cooled down. So most all the streets are black, the alleyways are black, the fences between homes and businesses are black, and even some of the homes themselves are made up of lava rock so they are black as well. The brightest spot in the whole city of Goma was in the churches and church meetings, where the women put on their beautiful long dresses and headdresses. The dresses are most certainly the most colorful, bright and bold of any dresses I had ever seen anywhere in the world.

We were taken by the pastors to our hotel, a beautiful old French era hotel with huge balconies, marvelous tiled rooms and king sized beds. Because of the security issues, we were established just a couple blocks away from the North Kivu State capitol grounds, so we felt a bit secure as we settled in for the night. The rooms were nice, even to the point of being luxurious, but the water works didn't work half the time, primarily due to the lack of reliable electricity, which didn't work half the time, which wasn't reliable due to the unreliability of the diesel powered generator, which also didn't work half the time. Well, you get the picture! It was a bit like camping out in a luxury hotel fit for a king.

We had a day to rest and then the pastor training meeting was to start on Thursday morning at nine. When the day of pastor training came around, we were all well rested and ready to go. Pastor Jacob, Pastor Isaiah, and the Goma area pastors would be teaching and preaching at the training sessions in the mornings, and then I would be bringing the message at the three crusade meetings. I was a bit disappointed we could not hold any outdoor meetings, but under the circumstances, the Full Gospel Business Hall that held a thousand people was about the best we could hope for.

The first day of the meetings started off with a bang, as over three hundred pastors from the Goma area showed up for the meeting. The local head of the pastors was Apostle James, and he was a giant of a man who had a very commanding presence, a deep voice and a wonderful grasp of the scriptures. He had rallied many of the pastors to come, and he was an excellent host and pastor. We had the blessing to visit his church on the other side of Goma for a ladies' teaching day on Saturday, a day when Pastor Jacob's wife gave the teaching.

The first day of the crusade I got up to speak and I started by praying for the city of Goma, for the protection of the Lord over the city, and I had two pastors from the audience stand in for the Governor of North Kivu, and for the President of the country of Democratic Republic of Congo. The President, who resides in Kinshasha on the western edge of Congo, had made several trips to Goma over the last few years because of all the infighting and rebel activity. It had been prophesied to me before I left Kansas to pray for these two men, as the key to the safety and security of North Kivu was to a great degree in their hands. Both are Christians, and the prophetic word for the Governor had to do with his personal walk with the Lord, and how the strengthening of his walk would lead the people of North Kivu to trust more in the Lord as well.

The Lord has prophesied over me through a lady at a conference in Kansas City that winter before the Goma meetings. The conference was in a packed auditorium of several thousand people, and as I took my seat in the only empty chair I could see in the hall, the Lord had seated me beside a lady with a prophetic mantle. She was African-American, and after we had visited for just a few minutes, she asked if she could give me a word of prophecy. I said, "Of course," and so she started to prophesy over me. She said, "The Lord says, I am going to shoot you out like an arrow out of My bow, and the point of the arrow is going to be burning with fire." And the Lord says, "Everywhere I shoot you, you are going to hit the bulls eye of the target and catch the target on fire!" So I thanked her for the prophecy and felt it was a very particular word for the upcoming mission I would have in Africa, not knowing at that time that I would be going to the Congo.

So as I relayed that word to the people of Goma, I was speaking in English and the translator was giving the message to the people in French, which is the official language of the Congolese. In addition to those two languages, there are many who speak Swahili, and their individual tribal dialect, of which there are over two hundred in the whole of DROC. I told the people of Goma, "I have come over ten thousand miles to visit you, and I am on a mission to bring a word from the Lord to you, and to catch the city of Goma on fire." It was a mighty declaration and received with great warmth by a group of people who were desperate and hungry for some encouraging news after all the gloom in their surrounding circumstances.

After the first two days of meetings, however, very few people came forward to make a decision to accept Jesus as Lord, and the evangelist calling in me was starting to get more than a little frustrated. I always want to see people get saved, but because of the nature and the location of the auditorium, very few unchurched people came into the hall. The audience was almost one hundred percent already churched people; we were having good crowds and some fabulous choirs from the area churches, but few decisions. A handful of people came forward for healings or to rededicate their life, and one lady was dramatically set free of some kind of demonic oppression, but for the most part the meetings were noteworthy for their lack of anything significant to report. Everything was a bit too tidy and proper for my liking.

So Sunday morning rolled around and I was beginning to boil over with frustration. Not only were the meetings rather mundane, but we had also gotten frustrated with the camping out issue at the old French hotel, so on Saturday we packed up and moved to another hotel on the east side of Goma, a hotel that sat right on the shore of Lake Kivu. This second hotel was much more to our liking; the food was excellent, the electricity and water works were much more reliable and best of all, the scenery on the shore of the big lake was absolutely stunning.

Lake Kivu is a huge lake that was formed by the lava flow damming up a river in centuries past that had flowed down the valley below the base of Mt. Nyiragongo, and the lake had now been backed up to form a great body of water over one hundred miles long, and several miles wide in places. It is rimmed with mountains and villages and on the northeast side by Gisenyi and Goma. Ferries and fishing boats traverse the beautiful, blue body of water, and the contrast between looking out over it and the despair of the city of Goma certainly lifted our spirits.

Though the hotel accommodations had improved dramatically, I was still perplexed by the question, "What exactly am I doing here, Lord, why did you bring us all this way for no decisions and no real visible breakthroughs?" Not only that, but on Saturday night I had gotten sick, from either some bad food or just battling in the spirit realm, so when Sunday morning dawned I wasn't feeling too chipper, and in fact was wanting to back out of my Sunday morning speaking engagement at a local Goma church. But then two things happened that turned my day around, and gave me hope for the final day of the crusade. First, Anna, Pastor Jacob's wife came down at breakfast, where I was drinking tea and toast trying to nurse my upset stomach, and she said, "I have been noting your growing frustration with the situation here in Goma, and the Lord gave a word to me for you last night." I said, "Good, I want to hear it, I'm starting to feel like that volcano over there, I'm about to boil over with frustration here in this place!"

She said, "The Lord says to you, "Just do what I called you to do, I brought you here to preach the word and bring the fire. Just do what I called you to do and I will take care of the rest!" So I told her, "Thank you very much, I was certainly needing that," as the word gave me great encouragement, knowing that I was still on track and that God was aware of every detail of the situation we were in. He was basically saying, "The battle is not yours, I have your back and this one is under control!" How often I have been guilty of trying to do the Lord's work, especially in Africa where no matter how much preplanning, it always seems as if nothing goes quite according to plan.

The second thing that happened that morning was just as I had made up my mind I wasn't going to go preach at the local church, Apostle James showed up with a car at nine in the morning and said, "The people are waiting for you," as if to say, "you're not going to get out of this one." Even though I was weak and faint and my stomach was doing cartwheels, I piled into the car for the rough trip across Goma. It seems we hit every lava rock and crater in the city streets as we wound our way down several back alleys towards the church.

When we got to the church, there were about four hundred people, shoe horned into a building on one of the back alleys of Goma, and the high praise and dancing were well underway, with the sweat beginning to roll as the heat inside the building built up.

I sat down with a couple of pastors near the back window, hoping to catch a breath of fresh air as it rapidly exited the room; although the Holy Spirit and the glory of the Lord were filling the place, fresh air was definitely in short supply. I was still feeling very faint and sick as I was introduced and came up to the platform to speak, and as I started to speak I felt like I was going to fall over, so I just spoke to the people, "I am going to get down on my knees and pray," and so that is what I did! I got down on my knees in front of four hundred people who were waiting to hear the message this visitor from ten thousand miles away was going to deliver to them. As I was on my knees, I just kept asking the Lord, "Lord, give me strength to stand, give me air to breathe."

After about five minutes on my knees, I felt a fresh breeze of the Holy Spirit blow across me. It was unmistakable in its intent to encourage and strengthen me, so I got back up and with renewed vigor began to speak. It ended up being a great day for the Lord's church and for me. Before I left that afternoon, I had preached for an hour and a half, and before leaving laid hands on and prayed for every single man, woman, and child in that place! It was a miraculous turnaround from how I had felt when I arrived to preach that morning.

Three o'clock in the afternoon came around pretty quickly, and after taking a short rest at the hotel, we were back in the car and on our way to the Full Gospel Hall. The words of the prophecy kept ringing in my ears, "The Lord says, you just preach the word and I'll do the rest." I was more than willing to let the Lord do His part, I was still feeling weak from the battle with sickness the night before, and I was very happy to let the Lord have the battle. The Congolese are great musicians and have some of the finest choirs, and after listening to them and joining in the praise and worship for an hour, we were all lifted up in spirit and felt like it was going to be a grand finale, a night to remember. The hall was filled, and there were even a few people sitting on the outside; the ladies were all dressed in their brightest Sunday best, and everyone was beginning to move in the spirit and dance a bit to the Lord.

The Lord had given me a special message to preach to the people of Goma this night, a message right out of the book of Second Chronicles of the Bible regarding great spiritual warfare, and trusting the Lord to fight the battle for us. It was the story of King Jehoshaphat and how the enemies of Judah and Jerusalem, a great multitude of enemies from Moab and Ammon, and others with them, came to do battle against Jehoshaphat. The story unfolds in Second Chronicles chapter twenty, and says, *"And Jehoshaphat feared, and set himself to seek the Lord, and he proclaimed a fast throughout all Judah."* (2 Chronicles 20:3)

Jehoshaphat had the natural reaction that anyone in his situation would have; he was full of fear, just as the people of Goma were. But he fasted and prayed and cast his burden upon the Lord, and in his weakness, he cried out to the Lord, "O, our God, will you not judge our enemies? For we have no power against this great multitude that is coming against us; nor do we know what to do, but our eyes are upon You." Then the Lord blessed Jehoshaphat with the words of a prophet, Jahaziel, who was sent to speak to him to give him the plan and strategy of the Lord in the upcoming battle. Jahaziel spoke to the king and said, *"Thus says the Lord to you: Do not be afraid or dismayed because of this great multitude, for the battle is not yours, but God's."* And Jahaziel went on with the specifics of the strategy, *"You will not need to fight in this battle. Position yourselves, stand still and see the salvation of the Lord, who is with you, O Judah and Jerusalem! Do not fear or be dismayed; tomorrow go out against them, for the Lord is with you."* (2 Chronicles 20:12,15,17)

And so according to the words of the prophet, King Jehoshaphat appointed those who would sing, and those who would praise, and they went out before the enemy army saying: "Praise the Lord, For His mercy endures forever." And the culmination of that word the Lord spoke through Jahaziel, and the ensuing battle, was that *"when the people began to sing and to praise the Lord, the Lord set ambushes against the people Ammon, Moab, and Mt. Seir who had come against Judah; and they were defeated."* (2 Chronicles 20:22)

The parallels and similarities between the story of Jehoshaphat and people of Goma were unmistakable; the Lord had given me this message because He wanted the people of Goma to know the battle was not theirs, and that they need not shrink back in fear. If they would just listen to and heed the words of the prophet, the Lord would deliver them from the hand of the enemy. The Lord was also saying that the weapons of their warfare were not carnal, as in troops, guns, and ammunition, but the weapons were mighty in the spiritual realm. The Lord was just saying to the people of Goma, "If you will raise up an army of those who would praise and worship Me, I will cause the enemy to ambush each other and deliver you."

As I got up to speak the same words as Jahaziel had spoken to the people of Judah, something began to happen in the spirit realm that was amazing and yet remarkable in its power. After preaching this message for an hour or so, I invited the worship band to start to play, and I began to exhort the crowd to raise up a radical time of praise and worship to the Lord. People were starting to move about, some were crying out to the Lord with their hands lifted high, some with tears running down their faces and some clapping and singing with the praise band. I continued to exhort for a few more minutes, and then something broke loose in the spirit realm, and every saint and timid and shy person in that hall just began to come undone in their exuberant praise!

As the cascade and volume of praise escalated, an even more amazing thing happened: a visible glory cloud came into the hall and filled the place, the glory of the Lord was in the place, and the tears and worn down faces all turned into faces of joy and shouts of praise and laughter! Many of the men took off their suit jackets and coats and began to wildly wave them in circles over their head, and scores of women broke out in riotous tribal line dances, casting all their burdens and cares onto the Lord as this pandemonium broke out all over the hall. I was still standing on the platform, dancing about myself, encouraging the people to abandon everything in praise to the Lord, which they seemed to be doing.

I was awestruck as I watched it all unfold, I had never seen anything quite like it here on this earth; the glory cloud, the people all dancing and rejoicing in a crescendo of more and more noise and radical praise. This all went on for about twenty minutes, but because we were running up against the permit time to exit the building, the Apostle stepped in and finally things began to slowly settle down and get back to "normal." Everyone was exhilarated and at the same time shaking and weak, it was a time of great energy expenditure and pouring out.

The amazing thing about the Lord's strategy played out in the week to come; the last meeting of the crusade was filmed by the pastors' association film crew, and so when we realized after it all happened what an amazing time it had been of God establishing and confirming His word to us, we took the film down the next morning to the local Immanuel Television broadcast studio. They played it out over their broadcasts several times the next week. And so God took that meeting in the Full Gospel Hall, and blew it up all over the Immanuel TV channel to reach homes in North Kivu, eastern Rwanda, and eastern Uganda, essentially reaching tens of thousands of homes. The Lord certainly works in mysterious ways, and His ways are without question higher than our ways.

In the days and months to come I began to realize

how profound an impact that meeting had on the city of Goma and North Kivu. Just as in the days of Jehoshaphat the word of the prophet had changed the destiny of the people of Judah, so too, the destiny of Goma and the whole of the DROC was changed when the people were obedient to the words of the prophet. As we exited the Full Gospel Hall and returned to the hotel, it was with a great sense of fulfillment and great accomplishment. Though the manifestation of the declared word was still a ways off, there was a sense of release in knowing the battle was truly the Lord's.

Monday dawned a new day, and we were supposed to meet the Governor and his staff to discuss economic trade issues, and just to greet him and present him with gifts. I had been given a prophetic word for the Governor, so I had the word written on a piece of paper in a sealed envelope, along with a couple of books that I had purchased for him, so I had all that ready to present to him. We were disappointed to learn that as a result of the rebel warfare, the Governor had been called out to a meeting in Kampala, Uganda, and he would not be able to meet with us as was scheduled.

But we were able to meet with his staff, and all of our team of five sat down together around a huge table in the ornate capitol building to exchange gifts and at that time I presented the prophetic word to the Governor's Chief of Affairs, and he in turn gave it to the Governor upon his return to Goma. Because brother Mark was on our team, and was the Governor's cousin, we had a fair amount of latitude to discuss an array of topics in the meeting. I also learned that the Governor was a Christian, so it dovetailed very well with the word that the Lord had given me for him, concerning not only his personal walk with the Lord, but also how he was to lead his people as the head of North

Kivu State.

As we left Goma on Tuesday, we were sorry to have to say goodbye to those precious people, leaving them in a place of what seemed to be, to the natural eyes, a place of impending doom and peril. Yet I felt the Lord was going to do something great and mighty to deliver Goma, we just had to trust Him and see His word come to pass.

We crossed the border back into Gisenyi, Rwanda, the next morning at nine, and then a couple of the pastors took us to the small airport on the outskirts of town, where we hopped a small plane for the flight to Kigali. From Kigali we switched planes and from there flew back on Kenya Airways to Nairobi. All in all it was quite an adventure to say the least, and the fulfillment of the prophetic word, the best part of all, was still yet to come. One of the words in the story of Jehoshaphat kept coming back to me, where the Levites spoke to him just before the battle began, saying *"Believe in the Lord your God, and you shall be established; believe His prophets, and you shall prosper."* (2 Chronicles 20:20)

Upon arriving back in Kansas two weeks after the Goma crusade, I was very anxious to keep up on the events in Goma, to see how the Lord's word was going to be established. Brother Mark had stayed on in Goma to take care of some business, then he went back to Nairobi and was there in the fall when I got this email from him: "Jim, the rebels have entered the city of Goma, and have taken over all the government buildings and the financial institutions, and the Governor and his family, along with some other of the city officials have fled for their lives."

To say that I was disappointed and crushed would be the understatement of the year; I was depressed for days after receiving that email, almost to the point of being angry with the Lord. I was certainly questioning Him in my prayer time, asking repeatedly, "Lord, how can you abandon your precious saints in Goma, when the prophetic word said if they believe His prophets, they will prosper?" I found out later the thousands of United Nations troops did not engage the rebels or fight against them in any way, it was not in their mandate to engage or defend the city of Goma, they were just there as "peace keepers," whatever that meant. And so there was no real defense of the city, just a standby to prevent any wholesale slaughter or humanitarian crisis.

I just did not understand what the Lord was doing, it made no sense to me at all. So I did what every good prophet and believer does, it was really all I could do, I just waited on the Lord to see what would happen next. But it is the waiting that is always the difficult part. One thing about the Lord I have learned is this: His timing is always perfect, and He always has His reasons for doing whatever He is up to. After a week went by, I had been in much prayer and travail about the situation in Goma, as I am sure many of the saints in Goma had been as well. To my surprise I received another email from Mark, and it was a shock to me as I opened it and read: "Brother Jim, you won't believe this but the rebel army has picked up and left Goma and turned the city back over to the government officials, and my cousin, the Governor, and his family have moved back into the Governor's mansion. Besides all that, the President in Kinshasha and the rebel leaders are in negotiations to try to meet some of their demands, and to come to a long term agreement about the future of Goma and North Kivu."

International pressure and the realization that they really didn't want to govern the city of Goma also played into the decision by the rebels to exit the city, but for whatever the reason, the results were joyful, something I could certainly get behind, and once again I was starting to shout, "Bwana Asifiwe!" when thinking about Goma and the Lord. "Maybe the Lord knows what He is doing after all," I confided to myself after my prayer time, laughing at my desire to control the Lord and tell Him how to take care of His business.

A few months went by and there was no news from Goma, other than an occasional news report saying the negotiations were still going on between the government and the rebels, but there had been no lasting agreement that I had heard of, so the peace was fragile at best. But then a breakthrough came; reports from the British Broadcasting Company and other news agencies said there had been agreements made in the negotiations, and about that same time I received another email from brother Mark, exclaiming, "Jim, you won't believe this but the rebels are out in the country pouncing on each other, killing each other in disputes among themselves." Needless to say, I was elated and fist pumping into the air, proclaiming the goodness of God.

So God showed me a very important kingdom principal with all that transpired at Goma; declare and decree a thing and it shall be established. When the prophet Jahaziel spoke into Jehoshaphat's situation, he spoke the words of the Lord, that the battle belonged to Him. When people believe and decree the words of the Lord, whether in Jehoshaphat's time or in 2012, it is then God's responsibility and obligation to carry out His word. All we have to do is keep believing in faith, keep praying, and stand back and let the Lord do His work.

As I think about the opportunity we were given to affect the destiny of Goma and North Kivu, it is very humbling indeed to have been used by God in the way that only He could have conceived. We went in and birthed the word of the Lord, the people believed, and the Lord brought it to pass. What an amazing adventure! I didn't fully realize the scope of it all until I went back to Goma in September of 2014 and saw all that God had done in the two years since I had last been there. It was all very amazing, the peace and stability that was established in Goma in that two year time period, when to the natural eyes they looked to be on the brink of destruction. God is good, all the time!

CHAPTER 12

Mumias Crusade 2012

I was planning to go back to Mumias in west Kenya in September of 2012, we had a bountiful harvest the year before and Pastor Luke thought it would be a good place to go again for another year. In January I was fasting and praying about the situation, and the Holy Spirit said to "go for it!" As the spring came around and fund raising began, I knew this was God's will for me to go back to Mumias and continue the good work that we had started. Plans were for a three day crusade again, to be held at three in the afternoon, with pastor training and encouragement to begin at nine in the morning.

We were expecting about fifty pastors and a great time of worship and teaching, and plans were proceeding smoothly until I received an email from Pastor Luke one morning in July. He said in the email that a group of Muslims were coming down to surround his church every morning during the Ramadan fasting period, and they were intimidating the church. So he was having his church people come into the church each morning to pray prayers to Jehovah God to have His angels surround the church for safety and protection, as a counter offensive to the prayers of the Muslims. It was a dual of gods, just as in the story of

Elijah when he encountered the prophets of Baal on top of Mt. Carmel. (I Kings 18)

So when I came into the airport at Kisumu, Kenya, two hours south of Mumias, I was met by Pastor Luke and a couple other brothers from his church, I was very curious about how the situation regarding the Muslims played out. Pastor Luke explained it this way, "Well, nothing happened in any violent way, they just kept coming down each day and prayed their prayers around the church for the duration of Ramadan, and we kept bringing our people in to pray for protection. And thank the Lord, He did protect us. But then another evangelist came to town about a month ago, in mid-August, and the old devil manifested himself at the outdoor crusade that he was preaching, at the crusade ground down the highway from the church."

I listened intently as he continued telling about the group, "The very same group of Muslims who had been surrounding our church rushed the platform of the evangelist, and they chopped him with machetes and nearly killed him. In fact, he is still in the hospital now three weeks later, he was so badly injured." The image of the evangelist getting chopped with machetes sent chills down my spine, as the crusade ground where this had taken place was the very same ground where we would be holding our crusade in a couple of days. So I asked the pastor, "Brother, do you think we should hire some more security and get some really big guys to stand around the platform?" Pastor Luke looked at me with confidence and faith boiling up in his eyes, and then declared, "No, we are just going to trust in the Lord!" I laughed and replied, "Easy for you to say!" So feeding off his boldness, I said, "Okay brother, I am with you, we will go forward as planned and trust in the Lord!"

As the day of the crusade came about, a good crowd was gathered at the crusade grounds, the praise teams were taking their turns up on the platform and it was a glorious day. So far there was no sign of any disruptions or anyone who looked suspicious in any way.

We were all praying for protection and so far the Lord was answering our prayers. It was a beautiful sunny day in Mumias, hardly a cloud in the sky, but as the day unfolded, by four in the afternoon when I got up on the platform to speak, dark clouds began to roll in from the south and seemed to be taking dead aim for our crusade. Within ten minutes after I started to speak, the first gusts of wind began to hit the banners behind me, and in just a few minutes after that, dark, angry looking clouds came roaring over the top of us with violent winds of forty to fifty miles per hour, and then a gusher of torrents of rain were unleashed. I got soaked as I was standing on the platform, as I wanted to be the last one standing as the wet ship capsized. When I jumped off the platform and headed for a nearby car in which to take shelter, I thought to myself, "Well, the enemy got the victory today in shutting this meeting down."

After leaving the crusade grounds, we all gathered a couple hours later at the church for a revival meeting until nine that night, and the Lord moved mightily through Pastor Matthew and some of the other speakers there. Although I had been unable to speak or share any message with the people that day, I was grateful for the move of the Lord in the church where people were getting healed and delivered. After the service, we bounced home through muddy roads till we got to Pastor Luke's home, thankful that the roads were not so muddy we couldn't make it. The ladies at the farm home were waiting for us with a great meal of chapatis, ugali, greens, and chicken soup, and fresh pineapple for desert; it was a welcome feast after a long, wet day in town.

The next day dawned bright and sunny, and I woke up early at the sound of the roosters on the farm as they welcomed the dawn. I have come to appreciate the beauty and peace of the farm, it is a place of great haven from the warfare of the crusades and revivals in the church. As we took off for town and the pastor training session, scheduled to start at nine in the morning, we all had high hopes for a great day for the kingdom of God. After the pastor training session in the morning, and the lunch which was served to all the pastors and leaders in attendance, we all walked the half mile down to the crusade grounds in preparation for the crusade which was to start at three in the afternoon.

I was shocked when we arrived at the grounds about two thirty, because the whole area was covered with shelled corn about six inches deep, which was on tarps laid out on the asphalt tarmac. I asked Pastor Luke, "What is going on with these guys taking over the grounds, don't they know we are to start at three?" He replied with a laugh, "Oh, no worries brother, they will take care of it." About that time a big flatbed truck pulled up, and four or five workers jumped out and started to bucket the corn into large, white, plastic mesh feed sacks that must have weighed one hundred fifty pounds when full. In fact, they were so heavy, it took two strong men to pick up one sack, as a third moved in under it to carry it up the ramp on his back, and throw down on the bed of the truck. I stood in amazement as I watched them clean up all the corn, covering about half an acre of ground, with just the plastic buckets in the thirty minutes prior to the start of our meeting. That same amount of corn in Kansas would have filled about two semi-truck loads, and it would have taken augers and tractors, and all kinds of fuel and posturing of equipment. It was just an astounding display of the strength of these people, and their willingness to tackle difficult tasks.

We did manage to get started shortly after three, and after an hour or so of praise and worship and dancing to the Lord, led on by praise teams from several different churches, I got up on the platform to speak. I had been watching the clouds off to the south and east, and I could see there was a storm brewing in the not too distant horizon. Again as I started to speak, it seemed as if the clouds all of a sudden began to gather and get really dark and angry looking, and within ten minutes after I started to speak, the wind was starting to pick up, and the people in the crowd began to nervously look over my shoulder at the rapidly approaching clouds.

At that point it became a struggle to keep their attention, as everyone could see this meeting was soon to be a washout. Sure enough, within another ten minutes it was raining cats and dogs, the banner on the back of the platform was about to blow over, and the keyboard players were desperately trying to cover the keyboard and sound mixer to keep them from getting damaged. The people in the crowd were all dashing for neighboring businesses that surrounded the crusade grounds, and for a second day in a row the meeting was washed out.

Pastor Luke and I and several other people had ducked into the shelter of a small welding and fabrication shop just a short distance from the crusade grounds, and we sat in there half soaked, watching the rain come down in torrents for about an hour. Though I always appreciate rain, I was disheartened that I didn't get to preach, as I was really looking forward to that after the previous day's washout. Pastor Luke sensed my frustration, and said to me, "We'll go back to the church in a bit after the storm lets up, and you can preach at the revival tonight." I replied to him, "Thank you, my brother, I appreciate that gesture. I just wonder, is the Lord protecting me from something unknown here, by washing out this outdoor meeting two days in a row?" We never did find out the answer to that question. He certainly may have been protecting me, or it could have just been the cycle of the rains for that season, but after watching the rain come down in torrents for about an hour, it finally stopped to the point we could walk back to the church.

At the church revival, a packed church of about two hundred people had a lot of pent up energy to release because of the two days of washouts. I preached the message I had started at the crusade, and then Pastor Matthew and I start to minister to the people individually. After calling up people and praying and prophesying over them, a lady brought a young boy, about twelve years of age, to the front of the church and asked me to pray for him. She was speaking to Pastor Matthew in Swahili, and said to him, "My son, Jerry, has been insane since he was about six years old. We are not able to send him to school because he cannot do his school work, would you please pray for him? I believe God can heal him." As she left Jerry in our hands, I put my hands on his head and began to pray over him. All of a sudden, he just stepped toward me and hugged me and would not let go, and I in turn embraced him, and wrapped my arms around him in a full body hug. The power of the Holy Spirit was swirling all around us, and I could feel the healing fire go through me and into this young boy.

After we held each other for perhaps three or four minutes, all the while I was praying for him as was Pastor Matthew, suddenly Jerry just slumped to the ground like a sack of potatoes hitting the dirt floor.

He appeared to be totally lifeless, but I knew the demons that had been tormenting him had just left, and the Holy Spirit was doing a mighty surgical work on his young soul. I had a tallit, a Jewish prayer shawl that my daughter had gotten for me as a gift when she was in Jerusalem in 2008, which was draped over my shoulders as I preached at the revival. I took it off my shoulders and wrapped it around the head of Jerry as he lay lifeless there on the floor. As he lay there, we went on with the service, praying for people and prophesying for individuals as the Holy Spirit highlighted them to us.

After Jerry laid there for about thirty minutes, he began to stir and finally got the strength to stand up, still a bit woozy from being under the weight of God's glory. Pastor Matthew then began to ask him questions in Swahili; Jerry was in his right mind, and could answer every question asked of him with a coherent and sensible answer!

Finally, after a round of prayers spoken over Jerry to seal the victory that had taken place over the demons in his life, he was released to go back to sit with his mother, as the people of the church were wildly praising him and the Lord for the victory. It was a mighty display of God's power to heal, and reminded me of the scripture in Matthew, where Jesus set a young boy free who was afflicted and a lunatic, just as in the case of Jerry. (Matthew 17:18) It is so amazing to see God's awesome power in affect today, just as it was two thousand years ago!

Another lady in the church had on a dress that the Holy Spirit highlighted to me while I was finishing up with Jerry. Her dress had a repeating pattern of the Great Sphinx of Egypt on a bright orange background, and it stood out among the crowd of the women in the church. The sphinx is an obvious demonic sign, as the sphinxes are a lion's body with the head of a man, and the meaning of the word sphinx is "the terrifying one, or literally, the Father of the Dead".

When I saw that dress, the Holy Spirit immediately spoke to me and said, "Pray for that lady!" So I called her, along with three or four other ladies up for prayer, and after praying for the first three, I finally came down the line to her. I began to speak over her and bind up the demons in her life as the Holy Spirit directed, and all of a sudden she just got swept off her feet and catapulted back about six feet into the waiting arms of a woman standing behind her. The power of God just blew her right off her feet and destroyed the power of the devil in her life.

Just like Jerry, she laid on the dirt floor of the church, but only for a few minutes. Then she slowly got up, and as she came back up to stand in front of me, I prophesied over her about how the Lord was going to use her is a mighty way in the vocation that she was in, and in the church she was attending, which was in another city. And just before I sent her back to her seat, I said to her, "Oh, and by the way, get rid of that dress! It is a walking billboard for the devil." She was the last person that we prayed for that night, by that time it was getting close to ten in the night, and everyone was getting tired after all the activities of the day.

The next day, Sunday, we had another great church service, but we didn't attempt to have the afternoon session of the crusade, as it was very cloudy and rainy all afternoon, and we didn't want to have to go through what we had the previous two days. So the Mumias Crusade ended with the church service that Sunday morning, and I still wonder to this day if the Lord wasn't just protecting me from something, by having those washouts three days in a row. Only God knows for sure.

CHAPTER 13

Tororo Crusade 2013

I had met a Pastor John over in Mumias, Kenya the year before, who had come by bus two hours to meet me and invite me to come to Tororo, Uganda for a crusade and pastor training in his home territory. Tororo is a bustling city similar to Mumias, having a population of about thirty five thousand, a commercial and agricultural hub for the surrounding villages and farms. To scout out the situation, I asked Pastor Luke in March of 2013 to go to Tororo and check out the situation, to get better acquainted with Pastor John, and give his recommendation about the prospect of holding a crusade there.

Pastor Luke made the trip and came back to me with the glowing report, "it would be a great place for a crusade." We planned the crusade for the following September, so preparations were made and the money sent over to get everything in place for a three day outdoor crusade with pastor training in the mornings. A worship team from Malaba, and another from Mumias, would combine with the worship teams from Tororo to bring us some excellent praise and worship to start off each of the events. In addition, the young preacher from Nairobi, Pastor Matthew, was going to join us to do most of the teaching at the morning sessions. Pastor Matthew was a powerful, highly anointed preacher that I had met the prior year at Mumias when I was there for an outdoor crusade. He had a very strong prophetic gift, and even better yet, a great sense of humor that really kept the people laughing at his jokes and unique presentation of the gospel. By all appearances it looked like a great team was coming together for a powerful series of meetings.

Before I left Kansas for the flights to Africa, I was in the prison for my usual Friday night meeting, and two different men who had been praying for the Africa trip, came up to me with prophetic words that the Lord had given them in dreams. The first said, " The Lord showed me in a dream, Jim, that as you were standing on the platform to speak, two witches in bright, tribal dress came up to the edge of the grounds and they were planning to disrupt the crusade. But as they approached the platform, the power of the Holy Spirit came upon them and knocked them both down to the ground; they could not stand up under the anointing of the Holy Spirit!" As I listened to him relay the dream, I sensed in my spirit that he was speaking about Tororo, as I had heard it was an area of great witchcraft, as well as there was a significant number of Muslims and other pagan practices.

The second inmate then came up to me and he also had been given a dream from the Lord, very similar to the first inmate's dream.

In his dream, he said "Jim, I saw you preaching with many people gathered around you, and a group started to press in around you that have evil intentions. They were not there to receive the word of the Lord. Just when it looked as if they would rush the stage or try to disrupt you, giant hailstones came down from the sky and fell on them and knocked them out!" Again, I felt in my spirit that this was a similar warning to the first dream, that the Lord was giving me prophetic warning about traps and snares that the wicked were setting to try and deter and disrupt the good plans of the Lord. As I took off for Kansas City to board a plane for Detroit, then Amsterdam, then on to Africa, I pondered these warnings and hid them in my heart, and in my prayer time I asked the Lord to reveal the plans of the enemy to me.

My flight from Amsterdam took me to Kigali, Rwanda, then after a brief wait on in the plane while it sat on the tarmac, we were back in the air headed for Entebbe, Uganda. Images of Entebbe swirled up in my mind as we came in for a landing, I had remembered from years back about the Israeli hostages that were taken captive at the Entebbe Airport and the successful rescue by the Israeli Special Forces unit, a rescue that was widely broadcast around the world. I wondered what Entebbe would be like tonight, and for that matter, what would Uganda be like, as this was my first visit to the country. I was to be met in Entebbe International Airport by three pastors who were going to be taking me up to Tororo, on the east side of Uganda.

The three pastors included Pastor John from Tororo, the host for the crusade, Pastor Luke from Mumias who would be bringing the worship teams from Mumias and Malaba, Kenya, and Pastor Matthew from Nairobi, who would be doing the bulk of the teaching at the morning training sessions. As I came into the airport terminal at nine at night, the terminal seemed especially dark and dirty, or maybe it was the haunting memory of the Israeli hostage situation that was coloring my glasses. Whatever it was, I have to say I was very happy to see my brothers, their beautiful smiles lit up the poorly lit terminal as their bright, white teeth, and Holy Spirit greetings made me feel right at home. "Welcome to Uganda, they all chimed in at the same time, it is good to see you my brother!" It had been a year since I had seen the three, and it truly was very special to see them after the year of absence and traveling ten thousand miles to get to this place. We all embraced each other, visited for a bit, and then quickly went out to the car and took off for Kampala, where we would be spending the night.

Entebbe sits right on the north side of Lake Victoria, the largest lake in Africa and one of the world's largest fresh water lakes, with a surface area of over twenty-six thousand square miles. As we headed north towards Kampala, the capitol city of Uganda, the highway followed the north shore of the lake for quite a distance, and the fishy smell of the lake penetrated and hung in the air like a wet blanket.

Traveling in the dark towards Kampala, I was growing very tired as it was approaching midnight, and after two days of car and plane travel, my body was aching for a good night's rest. The distance to Tororo was about 4 hours from Kampala, too much to make in the night, so Pastor John had made arrangements to stay in a hostel that some friends of his owned on the outskirts of Kampala. Kampala, a city of about two million people, in the city and the surrounding environs, is a bit like a downscaled Nairobi, very busy, crowded, with cramped roads and car and truck traffic that had long since outgrown the infrastructure that was designed to carry it.

Rolling into Kampala past midnight, we found our way to the hostel, and quickly made our way into our beds for the night. I think I was asleep before my head hit the pillow, and I know I didn't roll over until the light of dawn at seven the next morning. After getting up slowly the next morning and heading to the dining area for hot tea and toast, Pastor John announced that we needed to get moving because there was a church meeting this afternoon in Tororo where he wanted me to speak. So the thoughts of spending a relaxing morning around Kampala went flying out the window as we were back on the highway by nine, headed north and east toward Tororo.

We journeyed for four hours across varied landscapes, ranging from tropical and humid around Kampala, to more grassland and small farms, and then as we neared Tororo, we went through some very dense and lush tropical forests. It was good to be back in Africa, the sights and the sounds, and most of all the beauty of the people; and so different from Kansas, for here the people were everywhere, in the fields, in the villages, on the roads on bicycles, motorcycles, and buses and on foot. In Africa you are never far from many people.

As we were passing through the heavily forested area, Pastor John said, "Keep your eyes open in this area, often times baboons come up and sit along the roadside, hoping to get something to eat from the passersby as they go through the area." Sure enough, within a few minutes we saw a few baboons, maybe three or four alongside the road where the forest was particularly dense and nearly touched the road. I had Pastor John stop the car so I could get out and take a picture, but the baboons quickly became frightened and went scurrying off into the cover. I didn't want to take a picture of their back ends just vanishing from sight, so I didn't get a picture, hoping that we would get back that way before the week was out. But it was certainly a sight for my Kansas eyes to behold, where about the most exciting thing we see in the plains of Kansas are pheasants and an occasional deer or wild turkey.

Upon coming into Tororo, we could easily see the most distinguishing landmark, a huge rock mountain, Tororo Rock that juts up into the blue sky a couple thousand feet over the bustling city of thirty five thousand. We pulled into the city right about two in the afternoon, and went straight to an outdoor church on the edge of town, where about fifty worshipers were waiting patiently for us to show up so I could speak to the people. I was barely half awake as I piled out of the car at the urging of the three pastors, jet lag was really starting to take hold of me. But I drank some water, slapped myself on the cheeks a few times, then got up to speak and told the saints how happy I was to be in Uganda, and how I was looking forward to the crusades and pastor meeting in the upcoming days. Everyone was in agreement this was going to be a great time in the Lord for Tororo, the local pastors, and for the village of Matindi, the village area north of the city where the crusade was actually to be held.

The next day we all loaded into the pastor's car and took off on the dusty, red road on the way to Matindi. We passed many farmers on the road, most of them on bicycles, on little one hundred twenty- five cc motorbikes, or many on foot. The fields also were alive with people, many of the women were in the fields turning up the soil with big mattock hoes, and the time to plant the second crop of corn for the year was upon them. And in other fields that had already been planted to corn, the farmers were cultivating out the small weeds in between the rows of corn, or some were planting rows of beans for a nitrogen boosting crop in between the rows of corn.

It was quite a sight to see all of the activity, so different from Kansas where there are very few people in the fields; instead the fields are home to a few big pieces of machinery and one or two people at a time. We passed through a couple of small villages and then came to Matindi, another small village at the crossroads of a couple dusty country roads. We turned in there and proceeded to the backside of the village, and as we rolled into an open space beside a church, there I saw the platform and the sound system set for the crusade. On another side of the open space, stood a big awning tent- like structure to shelter the people from the hot midday sun, where the pastor training and morning sessions were to be held.

As I surveyed the scene, I thought everything looked rather small in scale compared to what I had pictured in my mind; the small village, the small platform, the small grounds. But I harkened back to a scripture and teaching I had just read a few days before. The scripture, from the book of Zechariah in the Old Testament, I had just read and I think God was preparing me just for this moment, said *"For who has despised the day of small beginnings? But these seven (speaking of the eyes of the Lord) will be glad when they see the plumb line in the hand of Zerubbabel—these are the eyes of the Lord which range to and fro throughout the earth."*(Zechariah 4:10) The Lord was saying to Zechariah that the things which man sees often times seem too small and insignificant, but the Lord holds in great esteem, as in the start of the rebuilding of the temple.

The teaching I referred back to spoke about the humble beginnings of just about everything in the kingdom of God; Moses, the baby in a basket floating down the Nile river would eventually become the deliverer of the children of Israel; David, the shepherd boy who would take down the giant Goliath who was threatening and mocking the God of the Israelites; and Jesus, who was born in a lowly stable in a cave, in the midst of the donkeys and oxen, the Messiah King who would come to save all people from their sins. And so the Lord's words were echoing to me, "it may look insignificant to you, but to me it is very important."

By ten in the morning the sun was beginning to beat down on us quite hot, and people were eager to seek the shelter of the tent, but they were also hungry for the word. Pastor Matthew was giving some powerful teaching and praying for people, and his meeting went on till after lunch. There were many children in attendance, and the children were anxious to hear about the Lord and be prayed for as well. They were always first to respond and rush to the front of any meeting and altar call, to see their innocence was always so refreshing and uplifting. As I surveyed the dozens of children that came forward, I was reminded of something that had happened to me in Kansas City just before I got on the plane to fly to Uganda.

There is a prayer room in Kansas City called the International House of Prayer 24/7 Prayer Room, where they hold nonstop prayer, praise, and worship that has been ongoing now for fifteen years. What started as a small prayer meeting with just a Pastor and a few people, has now blossomed into dozens of prayer and worship teams, to form a seamless, continuous flow of prayers and worship, incense going up to the throne room of the Father, and is beamed across the globe via the internet live streaming. While sitting in the prayer room the Sunday afternoon before I was to depart from Kansas City on Monday morning for Africa, a prayer point was posted on the screen for the two hundred or so people in the prayer room on which to focus. The prayer point was this: "Pray for the children of Uganda."

When that came up on the screen, the first prayer point of the day for me after sitting in the prayer room for a couple hours, I just about fell out of my chair! I said to the Lord, "Lord, you are certainly keeping close tabs on me, of all the people and all the different directions everyone is heading upon leaving this place, you have singled out me and the mission to Uganda for special prayers. How awesome is that?!" And so as I sat here in Matindi watching the children stream forward, many without shoes or decent clothing, and many with skin diseases, eye diseases, and other nutritional deficiencies, I was in agreement with the Lord, "Yes, these poor children of Uganda really do need our prayers!"

As the crusade got underway that afternoon under a beautiful, blue African sky, it was a very special time for that area of Uganda, a time to build on the small beginnings. A crowd of maybe six or seven hundred people had gathered to hear the "man of God" from Kansas, the white man who had come ten thousand miles to give them a word from the Lord. I preached to them about the story of the rebellion of Korah, Dathan, and Abiram, when they had come against the leadership of Moses in the wilderness, and basically challenged him to prove that God had sent him to lead the children of Israel. Moses had them to come back to see him the next day, and he told them, *"the Lord will prove to you that I have been sent by him by doing something unusual that has never been seen on the earth before."* And God certainly proved Moses point by opening up the earth and swallowing the rebels alive. The Bible tells us they descended alive all the way into Sheol, or hell, and along with them went all of their families and their possessions. (Numbers 16:30,33)

I related to the people how a similar hole, a hole two hundred feet across and ninety feet deep, had opened up in Western Kansas, and God was reminding the people of Kansas that He was the one who held our fate in His hands, and that to see or hear about that hole should be a reminder to us of the fate of Korah and the other rebels who had come against God. As I wrapped up the message and called the people forward for the altar call, many came forward to repent and confess their sins, and to get their hearts right with the Lord before a hole opened up under them to take them down to Sheol. Of course the message was all largely symbolic and an allegory, but the point hit home, and as the worship team came up on the platform behind to raise up more worship to the Lord, the altar was filled with people crying out for healing and for salvation.

The amazing thing that happened right at the end of the service was that the Lord put his exclamation point and confirmation on the message in a very unusual way; in a practically cloudless sky that had been very hot all afternoon, suddenly a small cloud came rolling in and it started to rain, just a small, brief shower that lasted maybe five minutes, but it was so out of character for the day that I knew it had to be the Lord giving His stamp of confirmation and approval. As the worship team continued to raise their voices in a crescendo of praise, it was all very breathtaking; I knew the Lord was building on the small beginnings!

That evening as we drove back to Tororo on the dry, dusty roads of Uganda, I was struck by the beauty and the simplicity of the people who were walking or bicycling along the roads or working in the fields. Their lives seemed timeless in a way; outside of the clothing that covered their bodies and the occasional boda boda (motorcycle) that sped by, I imagined they were for the most part carrying on the same activities in which their ancestors had labored. They were planting the fields into beautiful crops of maize (corn) and beans, a companion planting that assured the grain crop would have the fertility that it needed to produce a large ear or even two. Other fields contained elevated ridges of long vines of sweet potatoes, and then next to them would be Irish potatoes, tomatoes, and raised beds of collards, kale, spinach, onions, and other varieties of vegetables too numerous to mention.

It was a regular buffet of food, a timeless rotation of planting and harvest, planting and harvest, fueled by the hard work and sweat of these precious people. They were poor by western standards to be sure, according to statistics forty per cent of the Ugandan people live on less than one and a half dollars per day, but their lives were unhurried. And in a strange sense that defied logic, many were full of joy. And yet too, in the midst of the toil was great poverty, sickness, and bondage to witchcraft, addictions, illness and despair.

We passed through several small villages on the outskirts of Tororo where the men of the village were sitting around in a circle, they were all sucking up some liquid from a large container in the center of the circle, through six foot long cane "straws," and I asked the pastor what they were doing. He said, "They make a traditional brew from cane and molasses and they gather here to drink and get drunk. They easily get addicted to it and get wasted day after day, sitting around in these circles." I prayed for the people as we went speeding by, hoping maybe some would hear about the crusade at Matindi and have a desire to come and be set free.

That night after a great supper of ugali, a cooked corn meal dish that is a standard all over Africa, collard greens, and goat meat soup, all cooked over a charcoal fire, I retired for bed early to be fresh and rested for the crusade the next day. I was staying in the home of Pastor John who with his wife and family, were very gracious to play host to me in their home. Their home was in a complex of small rooms that were all joined together with a ten foot wide courtyard separating two buildings of rooms; the outdoor toilet was at one end of the courtyard, and the whole complex was sealed in by high walls at the back and front to provide security against thieves at night. It was all very basic, but I wanted to stay there to experience the life of the common person in Africa, to get an idea of what the conditions were like for them.

About the middle of the night I awoke with the feeling that something was moving around my feet, and I thought that was quite strange, as I was in a bed by myself and had tucked the mosquito netting into the mattress sufficient to keep the mosquitoes at bay during the night. But to check things out, I sat up and kicked the cover off my feet, only to see a mouse go scurrying off the edge of the bed and out of sight right below my feet! I laughed and thought to myself, "This can't be, the man of God sharing the bed with a mouse!" So I got up and meticulously tucked the mosquito netting under the mattress, taking extra pains this time to make sure there was no place for the little visitor to get in, and then eventually drifted back asleep. That mouse was the first of two I encountered in a rather significant way on this trip; this first one in the dirt and dire poverty of eastern Uganda, the second within the confines of the spotless, stainless steel and glass of the Amsterdam airport. God was just showing me that His creatures are pretty adaptable and can get along just about anywhere.

The next day we made the trip back out to Matindi again, and expectations were high for a great meeting. Many people from the villages around Matindi came again for the pastor training, then after a lunch served to all the people the crusade started about three under the scorching sun of the Uganda sky. After a great time of praise and worship for over an hour, the worship bands took their seats and I got up on the platform to speak. The translations were going smoothly today, as the day before we had a bit of trouble at first because some of the villagers in attendance could only speak their native tribal language, and so they were unable to understand the message. I was speaking the message in English, which was then translated into the Ugandan country language, Lugandan. So after a bit of consultation amongst the pastors and some trial and error, we decided to go with a three way translation, from

English, to Lugandan, to the tribal language of the village of Matindi. The three of us speaking had to pay close attention and closely coordinate so the message would go forth smoothly and everyone would stay tuned in.

I preached a message on Jesus, "the Living Water," and the many people who were there were touched and visibly being moved by the Spirit of the Lord. After preaching for an hour or more, I called the worship team to come back up and join me on the platform, and so as they took their place behind me, they started to sing and dance to the Lord, as I gave the altar call for the people to come forth and declare their allegiance to Jesus Christ as their Lord, or to come and ask the Lord for healing for the many who had diseases and afflictions. As many started to move forward toward the platform, the most amazing thing began to happen; many who were walking toward the platform, with their hands raised in worship toward the Lord, just began to fall over! It was as if a giant broom was going through the crowd, just sweeping some people off their feet, and they fell to the ground in front of the platform!

As I watched the Holy Spirit move through the crowd and knock people over, I was just standing there awestruck, and marveled at the awesome power of God. The worship team behind me continued to sing and lift up a chorus of praise to the Lord, or otherwise we would all have be in compete silence and reverence to the moment. And then the Holy Spirit brought back to me the dreams the inmates had relayed to me before I left Kansas, and specifically one of the dreams, about giant hailstones coming down out of the sky to knock out the ones who were involved in witchcraft. This is what I was seeing before my very eyes, the Lord was confirming the dream that he had given; His power was greater than any power of the enemy, and God was proving it to the people who were in attendance that day! It was a powerful time, and many others who were left standing came forward for a confession of faith and for prayers for healing, and many gave their lives to the Lord and were healed as well as those who were delivered from witchcraft.

The next day was Sunday, and I was scheduled to preach at a church in the opposite direction than Matindi from Tororo, to the south at a small church where about one hundred people had gathered to hear the "white man from America." As I got up to preach, I asked the people how many had made it to the crusades, as I recognized some of the pastors at the church had been at the meetings. About half of the people raised their hands to show they had been there. Then I asked how many had received a healing or some kind of deliverance, and about twenty five people jumped up and formed a line at the front of the church to give a testimony. The testimonies were all very powerful, and spoke of the awesome healing power of the Lord, and the people were clapping and rejoicing and giving shouts of praise as the testimonies went forth. Toward the end of the testimonies a middle aged lady came dancing from the back of the church to the front of the line, and she took the microphone, all the while dancing to the Lord, as the joy just continued to bubble out of her.

She told her story of what had happened to her on Friday, the day the Spirit moved so powerfully in the midst of the crowd at the crusade. She said, "I was very sick that morning here in my village, I could not get my breath and felt like I was going to die. I struggled all morning to breathe, and when my friends showed up in a car to pick me up to take me to the crusade, they all told me, 'You should not even go, you are probably not even going to make it to the meeting!'" But I said to them, "I am going to go, and by the grace of God I am going to get healed, and if I die, at least I will die seeking the face of the Lord!"

And so with great faith she proceeded to go to the meeting, believing with all her heart that God was going to show up mighty for her. I don't remember seeing her out of the hundreds of people there at the crusade, but it was obvious that she made it there and that the Lord gave her a great healing. Not only could she breathe just fine, but she was dancing to the Lord on the way to the front of the church, and back to her seat as well. What great faith she displayed, and as I heard her testimony, I realized the reason we here in America rarely see those kinds of miracles is simply because the people don't believe and ask for them. The Lord says, "Ask and you shall receive!"

That Sunday afternoon after lunch, Pastor John told me he wanted to take me back out to Matindi, as there were some people there who wanted to say goodbye to the "man of God from America." So we headed out to Matindi about two in the afternoon, and rolled into the village one more time for what I thought would be a short and sweet goodbye with a few people. As we came in, I was shocked to see over five hundred people gathered there, sitting under the tarpaulin awning and a large tree next to the it, who were gathered to hear me speak one more time, and to receive a blessing and goodbye from me. With no sound system and straining to have myself heard by the crowd of people, I preached and exhorted to them to be faithful to the Lord, to keep believing for all the promises that He had given them in His word. Many of those who were there were children, from infants nursing at their mama's breast, to teenagers who were there with their families.

As I surveyed the children, many barefoot and with very poor clothing, some with obvious eye and skin diseases, the Holy Spirit reminded me of the prayer point of focus at the International House of Prayer in Kansas City: "Pray for the children of Uganda!" Here they were, and I was before them one more time before leaving these precious people. After speaking to them for an hour or so, I had the pastors help me to line the people up, and then each one filed by in front of me where I laid hands on them and prayed blessings over them, after the pastors had anointed them with oil. It was a bittersweet goodbye, as I hated to leave but knew that I had to, as I had scheduled appointments and meetings in Nairobi beginning on Tuesday of the next week. But before I got in the car the villagers had a gift for me as well; two very healthy, live chickens were given to me to take back with me to Tororo. I donated the chickens to the pastor's wife later in the evening, and I think we had them with the ugali and greens we had for supper that night. Talk about farm to table!

The next day Pastor John took me to the border of Busia, Kenya, on the border between Kenya and Uganda, where he let me out to board a matatu minibus at the central bus stop in Busia. I wanted to see some of the countryside between Tororo and Kisumu, Kenya, where I would be boarding a commuter jet for the flight to Nairobi. As I was sitting in the matatu waiting for the trip to begin, a man who worked with another bus at the station came up to talk to me, I'm sure he had noticed I was a white man and most likely an American.

As he was standing talking to me, he noticed a nice ink pen I had in my shirt pocket, and he said to me, "Would you mind if I borrowed your pen for a minute, I need to check off the passengers who are getting on the other bus?" I answered back to him, "No, I don't mind, I just need it back before my bus leaves in a few minutes." And so I loaned him my nice ink pen that I had bought in America especially for the trip. After about fifteen minutes, I knew we were getting close to departure time, and I went over to where he was standing and asked for my pen back. He replied, "No problem, no worries, I will bring it to you in just a minute." The minute passed, then two minutes, then five, and then the bus fired up and we were off minus my now stolen ink pen.

Later in the week, when I got up to speak at the student kesha in Nairobi, the first story I told the students was how I had my pen   stolen by the bus company worker out in Busia. Although it was somewhat of a humorous story, and the students got a good laugh out of it, it was also a prophetic act. Because corruption is such a big part of life in Kenya, and all over Africa where I have traveled, God has called me to confront and call out corruption everywhere I go to preach. And so I had barely crossed over the border and into Kenya, when already someone had stolen something from me. God was just highlighting to me the extent of the corruption that runs through every facet of the society, from business people, to all levels of government, and even among some of the pastors of the churches. The spiritual battle was on!

CHAPTER 14
Nairobi Kesha 2013

When I got to Nairobi, I held an all-night kesha, a praise and worship and preaching session, with students from several universities, and the students got a great laugh out of the story of the stolen ink pen. The fact that the "man of God" from America had come to Africa to not only preach the gospel, but to take on, root out, and help dispel corruption from Kenya and other African countries, and now the very first thing that happened to him inside the Kenya border was something was stolen from him! That was a prophetic act that spoke volumes to me about the state of affairs in the country of Kenya.

The kesha all- night prayer vigil is part of the rich heritage of religious traditions practiced by nearly all Christian denominations and churches in East Africa. They are especially scheduled around Christmas or Thanksgiving time, but are appropriate at any time of the year. The usual program or schedule goes something like this: it begins about seven at night with exuberant praise and worship and dancing, then is followed by the first preaching and testimonies beginning about ten, then more praise and worship, another round of preaching and testimonies beginning about three in the morning. A final round of praise and worship and a breakfast ensues about five or six, when all the people head for home and a good "night's" rest. Interspersed throughout the night are times of individual and corporate led prayers; for the country, its leaders, the churches, or anything else that is on the hearts of the people involved.

The students were adamant that we should have an all-night kesha on Friday night, and then come back to the same auditorium for a church service on Sunday, with a trip to Daystar University in east Kenya on Saturday, sandwiched in between the two Nairobi meetings. It was going to be a busy schedule; I knew I was going to need the grace of God to be able to keep up with the university students through the whole weekend, but I agreed to the schedule and looked forward to the meetings.

When Friday night came around, I was well rested and ready to go, in anticipation for what the Lord was going to do that night. The meeting got underway promptly at seven and started off with a bang, with a couple hours of praise and worship and dancing. It is such a joy to watch the African people dance to the Lord and praise Him with such radical exuberance, especially for the eyes of this Westerner, where in America so many church services are rather staid and stifling. The students had a small praise band going with a keyboard, drums, and a guitar, and then a chorus of about six singers. They kept a steady drumbeat of praise and worship going, while the rest of the students danced with the heart of King David when he was dancing before the Lord, as the ark of the Lord was being brought back into Jerusalem.

The best of them would come to the front and lead in the singing, or a group would come forward to lead the dance, and they would go on with one song or chorus for fifteen or twenty minutes, then others would come forward to lead.

Africans love to line dance as well, and so at certain points, or to accompany certain songs, line dances would break out and begin to form a human chain that snaked around all the chairs. One dance even went out one set of doors at the front of the room, down the hallway to the back end of the room, and back into the auditorium through the back set of doors! I joined in to the best of my ability, and the old saying "White men can't jump" was certainly in play, as I was struggling to keep up and keep in rhythm with these people who seemingly invented the beat and rhythm. It was a joyful time before the Lord!

I got up to preach about eleven that night, and preached for two and a half hours, that was just my time with no interpretation, as these students all were fluent in English. At the end of the preaching time I had an altar call for those who wanted to give their life or rededicate their life to the Lord, and several responded to the invitation. Then the Lord gave me a word of knowledge about someone who had been given the apostolic or missionary calling, and they had not responded to the calling as the Lord wanted them to do. I waited about a minute and then repeated the word of knowledge, as I was confident in what the Holy Spirit was saying to me, "Someone here has been given the apostolic calling and you have stuffed it, you are not moving forward into it as the Lord would have you to do."

After another half a minute delay that seemed like an eternity, a young man named Titus, who was sitting at the table of honor beside me, and who was my roommate in the hostel where I was staying, got up to come forward for prayer and receive the word of knowledge. He had been with me from the time I had arrived in Nairobi the previous Tuesday, and he had been my faithful shadow to follow me everywhere I went in Nairobi. He was with me to protect me, as well as getting me access to a computer and office space in the Strathmore University where he was a student. But he had never mentioned his calling or anything about his spiritual walk, he was most known as an outstanding soccer player who was attending Strathmore on a soccer, or "football" scholarship.

So as Titus came forward, I was both surprised and pleased that the Lord had something for this outstanding young man, a student leader in every regard, and he was courageous enough to come forward for prayer in reference to the word. As he came forward, he was a bit tentative; every eye of the students in the auditorium was upon him, and he came and stood beside me as I handed him the microphone.

He started to talk about his apostolic calling. "I was at a revival meeting with my grandmother when I was seven years old; there was an evangelist that came to our village in west Kenya. He held some powerful meetings, and at the last meeting, he gave an altar call for salvation decisions, and then he also called up anyone who wanted to be sent to the nations to preach the gospel, to receive the calling of the Apostle Paul. I was so touched by the Spirit of God; I went forward to be prayed for to receive the calling. I have now come to Nairobi to play football and get my degree in business, but I have known deep in my heart that I am to take up the mantle of the apostle and go to the nations to preach the Word. I know that is what God wants me to do!"

You could have heard a pin drop among the two hundred or so students in attendance, no one made a sound as he made his confession of desire to rededicate his life to the calling. I listened to him speak and as he finished, I laid my hand on his head and prayed for the Lord to stir up that desire that had been given to him when he was seven, and walked forward with boldness by himself into unknown territory. When we got back to the hostel that next morning, I encouraged him some more to go for that highest calling that God had placed in his heart.

The kesha was a very powerful time of crying out to the Lord in prayer and worship. After a snack of hot tea and sweet bread about one in the morning, I picked up the guitar and started to play one of my favorite worship songs, "There is Power in the Name of Jesus, to Break Every Chain." The worship band began to chime in, first the keyboard, then the choir, and eventually all the students in the place were singing at the top of their lungs, "Break Every Chain." It was so powerful it just about lifted the roof off the place! That song and others went on for about an hour, and then the second preacher got up to speak at three that morning. Pity the second preacher on kesha night, by this time people were starting to get sleepy and really fighting the desire to drift off.

But we all hung in there with a bit of nodding off, and we finished off the night with more prayers, some more worship, and a sense of purpose fulfilled in keeping the fire burning all night. When breakfast was served at five in the morning, it was a welcome sight to see more hot tea, cakes, and eggs to brighten us up and get us going on our way to our respective homes. Little did we know of the events to come that day in Nairobi that would not only shake Nairobi but the whole world. The Lord had us positioned at the kesha to lay down a foundation of prayer the night before the infamous Westgate Mall terrorist attack, which unfolded that very day only three miles from where we were up all night at the kesha.

After heading back to the hostel, we all quickly jumped into bed for a few hours of sleep before we were rudely wakened at eleven to get ready to go out to Daystar University, two hours east of Nairobi.

When my roommate tapped me on the shoulder and told me it was time to get up, I couldn't believe the five hours since I jumped into bed had sped by so quickly. What a rush! I got up and jumped into the shower to try to wake up and get a little fire going inside of me, but I had to admit it was a struggle to get going. But after the shower and some more of that good hot tea with milk that is so often served in Kenya, I was starting to come around and get excited for the trip to Daystar. My ride to go to Daystar was with Mark, the Congolese brother who had helped set up our trip to Goma in 2012. He was a student at Daystar University, studying communications and information technology with the ultimate idea that he would go back to the Congo and work for the government in the information technology business.

Daystar University is a Christian liberal arts university that has a campus in Nairobi as well as a new campus at Athi River, Kenya, which is where our team of five was headed. After fighting through some intense traffic jams that had us sitting for what seemed like an eternity, we finally broke through on the Mombasa Road and sped towards Athi River and the University for our two o'clock appointment. As we went on out into the country past Athi River, we turned off the main highway and bounced over rough and rocky roads for a couple miles before we came to the campus. I was amazed as I surveyed the campus; I was struck by the isolation, the peace, and the beauty of the campus, set down in the Kenyan bush with beautiful wildlife and outcroppings of massive rock and brush surrounding the beautiful buildings. It was here that I would be speaking to the student leaders, the Christian leaders who will go forward to lead the next generation, not only in Kenya but in countries all over Africa.

As we pulled into the parking lot, we were met by some of the student leaders and the faculty sponsor of the Christian Leadership Fellowship, who were waiting inside the auditorium for the meeting to begin. It was a great meeting, and I exhorted the students to rise up to the call that the Lord had placed on their life, that the future of Kenya and all of Africa was in their hands. I encouraged them and gave them the word of the Lord to encourage them, where the Apostle Paul says in the book of Thessalonians, *"Faithful is He who called you, and He will see it come to pass."* (1 Thessalonians 5:24)

As I looked into the eyes of these young people and saw their sincerity and their yearning for a better future, free of corruption and the kingdom of the devil running the affairs of the African people, I wanted to impart in them the fire of the Holy Spirit. That fire had prompted me to come to Africa to preach in the first place, the fire that I had been given by the Lord to sacrifice and give up much comfort, to travel twenty thousand miles round trip to share with the African people the word of the Lord. It was a precious moment to stand before such innocence and purity, knowing that I may never be back to this place again, but I was thankful for the opportunity. So I finished the message and then invited the students to come down to the front for an impartation of the fire. Most all of them came, and I anointed them with oil, which is symbolic of the anointing of the Holy Spirit, and then prayed a brief word or two over each one individually.

CHAPTER 15
Westgate Mall Terrorist Attack

After the meeting we took a tour of the beautiful campus of Daystar, took some pictures of each other in front of various landmarks, and then headed over to brother Mark's apartment for a cup of hot tea. As we were relaxing in Mark's apartment, catching our breath after a day of rather intense meetings, suddenly a couple of the brothers began to receive text messages, and then news reports on their smart phones about a terrorist attack that was beginning to unfold back in Nairobi at Westgate Mall, an upscale mall just west of downtown Nairobi. The first reports were a bit sketchy, but it was apparent that something very dramatic and tragic was happening in the mall.

Reports indicated that a group of terrorists, the exact number not confirmed at that point, had taken over the mall and were holding many people hostage. As we headed back to Nairobi about sundown, it was with a heavy heart and somber mood that we got back to the hostel about eight. We had some hot tea and a quick supper, as we were still tired from the kesha the night before, but as we turned in for a good night's sleep it was apparent that the situation at the Westgate Mall was going to dominate the spiritual atmosphere for the rest of the weekend. At that point we just had no idea how much.

When I woke up the next morning, I felt somewhat rested and ready to go for another service. The plan was to have an all day long service back at the university auditorium where the kesha was held, and the service was going to start at nine in the morning and go until two in the afternoon, at which time we would finish up with a dinner for all in attendance. Before we left for the church service, I called a friend from Nairobi who had planned to go with us to the service. My friend, whose Christian name is Hope, had an amazing story all her own that connected me with her through the Kibera Crusade in 2011.

In September of 2011, on one of the nights of the Kibera Crusade, she was walking through the Kibera slum on the way to visit her brother a short distance away from the Kamukunji grounds where we were conducting the crusade. She was fully covered in her hijab, as most Muslim women in Kenya wear the traditional covering required by their faith. As she walked through the Kamukunji grounds, she heard the worship music as it flowed out from platform to the far corners of the grounds, and she decided to stop and listen.

After listening for a while, a white man from America got up on the platform and began to speak; the words that he spoke came from from God's word, and pierced her heart and began to stir up in her a desire to know Jesus and accept Him in her life as her personal Savior. It was a confirmation of a stirring that had been going on in her heart for quite some time, as she was full of questions and confusion about her Muslim faith, which had been her faith from birth. In fact, in her family were imams and leaders of the local mosques, so it was a momentous decision, a monumental turning point in her life, as she knew in her mind that this Jesus that was being preached was the answer that she was seeking, the answer to the stirring and the wooing by the Holy Spirit that had been going on in her heart.

She was changed from that moment and she knew she could not deny it, but she also knew that it was going to have profound ramifications for her life. To confess Jesus as her Lord and deny her Muslim faith would cost her everything; her marriage, her family, possibly her children, and maybe even her life. But she knew that to be true to herself, and honest with the stirring in her heart, she had to put everything on the line and say yes to Jesus, and so she did.

That man who was on the platform speaking that night in Kibera was me, of course, and through a circuitous series of events, I came to know this lady, Hope, two years later and heard the story of her conversion. I had met her earlier in the week at Strathmore University for lunch, to check up on her and see how she was doing in her new life as a baby Christian, and we had made plans at that time to go to the church service on Sunday with the university students. As I called her that morning to make plans to pick her up on the way to the service, her voice was very weak and failing, and she had only spoken a few words before she started to cry.

She began to tell me about one of her best friends in Nairobi who was in the Westgate Mall when the terrorists came in from the parking lot on the top floor. Her friend, a prominent radio and television personality, was seven months pregnant with her first child, and was at the mall to host a cooking demonstration at a restaurant on the top floor. When the Somali Islamic terrorists came bursting in and shot her, she was instantly killed and the baby in her was murdered as well, quite possibly the first two to lose their lives in the Westgate attack.

As I was listening to her cry on the phone, I realized the pain in her heart was twofold; not only was she grieving the loss of her good friend and baby, but also she was suffering because now that she knew Jesus as her Lord, she realized more than ever the utter demonic and senseless nature of the attack, perpetrated by people who were of her former faith. None of it made any sense, neither to her nor to me. I tried to speak some consoling words to her, but I could barely hold back the tears from my own eyes, and words in a situation like that are never adequate. I prayed with her, that God would give her the grace to forgive the attackers, and also for God to heal her heart from the pain she was feeling. And we also prayed for the family of her good friend, that they would be comforted in their time of immense grief.

It was for sure the low point of my time in Africa that year, as it was for many in Nairobi who had known only too well the capability of these people to kill and destroy. Nairobi had suffered through the attacks of Islamic terrorists many times over the years, the most notable attack was the bombing of the United States Embassy in Nairobi in August of 1998, when a bomb detonated near the embassy killed over two hundred people, and injured several thousand.

As we finished our conversation, she told me she could not go out to the church service, that there was no way she could go the way she was feeling at that time. I have to admit I did not want to go out myself; after several years of going to Kenya to preach, God had given me a heart for the Kenyan people, and the pain they were all feeling at that time was almost too much to bear. Americans could certainly relate when thinking back to the destruction of the World Trade Center towers in New York City, and the deaths of those who went down in the field in Pennsylvania, and into the Pentagon in Washington, D. C. It was all so senseless and shocking, and always provokes the questions, why, Lord? Why all the senseless violence and death? What hope is there for mankind, and why would God allow such destruction to wipe out innocent people?

As we took off for the church service, I was fighting back tears thinking about all the people in the mall who were losing their lives, and I was struggling to keep my head up. Reports were still coming out over the news channels about the ongoing siege at the mall; initial reports claimed there may have been as many as fifteen terrorist attackers involved. No one had any idea of the death toll, as it was impossible in the early stages to know how many of the thousands of shoppers were still in the mall, and how many had been able to escape into the safety of the many police and military units who were now stationed in a perimeter around the mall. Little did we know the siege would go on for several days, with the eventual death toll coming to sixty seven deaths, including four attackers, with many more injured.

There were also reports coming out about torture, that many of the victims had been questioned to see if they knew any Arabic language, or questions about Islam, and then the terrorists would kill or torture those who could not answer the questions properly. All we could imagine at this point was the worst, which this was going to be a tragedy of immense proportions for the people of Nairobi and Kenya.

Upon arriving at the university at nine for the morning service, I could see the reflection of my face in the face of the students who were beginning to gather there for the service. A look of fear, shock, and disbelief was in their eyes, and we were all dealing with, and fighting back the very same emotions. I didn't know if I had the strength to stand up and preach a message; after all, isn't God Himself under question in times like this? And yet I knew, and so did the students, that we could not afford to question God at this time, but the only thing we could do was just get down on our knees and cry out to Him, which is what we did.

As we cried out to Him in prayer, praying for the victims' families, and for those still trapped in the mall, and for the Lord to deliver us from the enemies, we began to gain strength. As the tears fell to the floor and our voices and prayers ascended to the throne room of God, we could also give Him thanks for positioning us on the wall of prayer and prophetic alert on the previous Friday night, when we labored in prayer and praise all night at the kesha. Of course we did not know what was forthcoming, but God certainly did, and the blanket of prayer laid down over the city may have in some small way mitigated the disaster at Westgate. Only God knows for sure the measure of all that.

We began to gain strength as we cried out together, and we lifted up praise to the Lord, and even got to the point where we could dance again. We could praise Him in the storm! And so we began to find joy in the midst of sorrow. I was reminded of Psalm 126, a song of deliverance and ascents, or rising upward, which quite accurately described the flow of the service that day. The Psalmist says: *"Those who sow in tears shall reap in joy. He who continually goes forth weeping, bearing seed for sowing, shall doubtless come again with rejoicing, bringing his sheaves with him."* (Psalm 126:5,6)

We had two special worship leaders who joined us that day, both highly anointed in their own walk, and they were able to help us ascend upward to the place where we could momentarily forget the sorrow that was going on around us. I got up and preached, and by the power of the Holy Spirit was able to encourage and exhort the group, to trust the Lord in every circumstance. Today was certainly a test of faith and for this day I believe we passed the test. After some more time of praise and worship we were beginning to cross over into the afternoon, and at two in the afternoon we closed the service and all sat down to enjoy a fine meal together, a time of fellowship and rejoicing in all that God had done that day, and that weekend.

After a good night's rest back at the hostel, Monday morning we began to make plans for a farewell dinner that night, for it would be my last night in Nairobi before getting on the plane to fly out to America on Tuesday night. I wanted to have lunch with Hope once more, to see how she was doing in the face of the pain she was suffering under, so we went to the west side of Nairobi to Java House Café, where we met for soup and salad. On the way to Java House, we passed not far from the Westgate Mall; the smoke was still billowing up from the mall into the warm Kenya day, as someone had set fires in the mall that eventually collapsed a large portion of the roof onto the floors below. The siege was in its third day, and though the government made claims about being in complete control, it was obvious that things were far from over. So the last impression I had of the mall and that whole scene, was looking back on it and seeing the black smoke billow up, wondering about the fate of those trapped inside. It wasn't for another couple of days that the military and the police actually took complete control and the attack was over.

That night I met with the student leaders one last time, for a time of toasting and reflection on the events of the weekend. We went to a local restaurant in Nairobi where we had a feast of goat meat, ugali, greens, and all the papaya and pineapple juice we could drink. We made several toasts to the success of the meetings, and prayed for another opportunity to do it all over again in the coming year. It was a memorable time, and looking back on that weekend, I am very thankful for the protection given to us by the Lord, as well as the grace to keep going in the face of hardship. But compared to those who had suffered in the mall, and the families of those who had lost their lives, we had nothing to complain about, and so I left Nairobi with joy in my heart for having fulfilled the calling of the Lord.

On Tuesday night of that week, I boarded the plane in Nairobi headed for Amsterdam, the first leg of the journey that would take me back to my home in Kansas. It was a bittersweet departure; it is always exciting to be "heading home," to sleep in one's own bed and eat food that is familiar to the palate and eye. But it was very bitter as well; as I felt the pain and sorrow the people of Kenya and especially Nairobi were feeling, in light of the attack on the Westgate Mall, which was still unresolved at the time of my departure. In a way, I felt as if I was abandoning my brothers and sisters from the universities who had battled with me in the spirit realm throughout the night at the kesha, only to have the battle manifest in the natural world in a horrific way much worse than any of us could have imagined. So I was starting to let down as is natural for a trip like this, where the warfare is so intense and the devil will do everything he can to tear down and wear down the opposition.

By the time I got to Amsterdam, after a nine hour flight where I was only able to sleep for maybe three or four hours, I was really beginning to weaken. My schedule allowed for a four hour layover until my next flight to Detroit, another eight hour flight that would be followed by another two hour layover, then a short flight to Kansas

City. The final leg of the journey was a six hour drive home to the safety of Western Kansas. After eating a breakfast in Amsterdam and checking my emails, I lay down on a padded seat in a quiet place and was just going to rest for a short minute, but rest I did.

I woke up with a start at 10:45 with my plane scheduled to leave at 11:15, I knew I was going to be in for trouble to make my flight. In a frenzy I dashed down to the boarding gate, only to be told the gate had been closed ten minutes ago and there would be no more passengers boarding. The attendants told me if I went up to the ticket service counter, I might be able to get another flight out that day to Minneapolis or Chicago, so I rushed up there hoping for the best, but to no avail. There were no empty seats on any flights headed out that day, so I was stuck with the prospect of spending the night in the airport, and having to pay another three hundred dollars for a change of departure date on my ticket.

It was certainly a stressful way to end the mission, and I was starting to come down with a respiratory infection that had me coughing and very congested, so I was hurting and down, both spiritually and physically. The good news was that I was in Amsterdam Schiphol Airport, one of the more beautiful and comfortable airports in the world, and that I had a day to loaf around the airport and just take it easy. So I just walked around the airport for a while, taking in all the sights and watching the people, sitting down occasionally to surf the internet or have a cup of coffee.

As I sat resting at a boarding gate area that was now vacant after a plane had just departed, the Lord gave me some comic relief that shed a different light on my situation. Out from under a heating fixture on the side of the wall at the boarding gate area came a mouse; he seemed to know what he was doing in that he made a sweep under all the seats in the area, looking for crumbs of food that may have fallen to the floor while people were in their seats waiting for the plane to depart.

The sight of that mouse running about in Schophol Airport, a place of stainless steel, acres of glass and sparkling tile, that is spotlessly clean and so efficiently run, really brought into perspective everything that had happened on the trip. I had recently been in the poorest of earthly circumstances in Uganda, where another mouse decided he wanted to share the covers of the bed with me, and now, here in this immaculate of all places, another mouse was making his living. I was somewhere in the middle, grieving for the pain of my brothers and sisters in Kenya, but the Lord was showing me He was in control of it all.

He was also reminding me of the mortality of all things here on the earth, that the lowest and highest of all creation would eventually pass away, and that he would replace it with a new heaven and new earth, where there would be no more tears, no more sorrow, no more pain, a place where death would not come. As I sat thinking about all that I had seen and been through the past month, all I could say in response to it all was, "Come quickly, Lord Jesus, come."

CHAPTER 16
Malaba Crusade 2014

The year 2014 brought with it new challenges and new opportunities, the Lord opened doors in places and ways that He had never done before. I had started off the year with a seventy day Daniel fast, a fast derived from the life of Daniel and a description given in the first chapter of the book of Daniel in the Old Testament of the Bible.

Daniel said to the steward whom the chief of the eunuchs had set over Daniel, Hananiah, Mishael, and Azariah (Daniel's Hebrew companions), *"Please test your servants for ten days, and let them give us vegetables to eat and water to drink. Then let our appearance be examined before you, and the appearance of the young men who eat the portion of the king's delicacies; and as you see fit, so deal with your servants." And at the end of the ten days their features appeared better and fatter in flesh than all the young men who ate the portion of the king's delicacies.* (Daniel 1:11-15)

While fasting and praying for open doors, I began to receive invitations from brothers over in Africa, inviting me to walk through open doors for kingdom advancement. One of the first to come was an opportunity to go to Malaba, Kenya, on the border of Uganda, with Pastor Luke and two Pastors from Malaba, Pastor Isaac and his wife Pastor Ellen. I had worked with Pastor Ellen the three previous years in

Mumias, Kenya, and Tororo, Uganda, and had found her to be a highly anointed worship leader and great woman of God. When she gets up on the platform to worship, she is standing before the Lord, and that is who she sings to! It was always a great joy to worship with her, and see her joy as she sings and dances to the Lord. He husband, Pastor Isaac, I had just met the previous year in Tororo, and he and I had an instant rapport as he described Malaba, and what he thought would be a great place for an outdoor crusade. And so as that invitation began to solidify, I decided to go to Malaba for a three day outdoor crusade and pastor training at the church of Isaac and Ellen.

By the time of the departure in early September, God had opened three doors of opportunity for me; the first, in Nairobi with the university students that I had been with for the kesha the year before, the second, the crusade in Malaba, and third, a trip back to Goma in the Democratic Republic of Congo, to follow up on the work done there in 2012. God had also put two very strong brothers to travel alongside me to Africa, and each was destined to be of great value to the mission before it was all finished. The first, Ronnie, was a young man from Kansas City who had been an inmate in the prison where I had been preaching. During a worship service one night at the prison, he got touched by the Holy Spirit and ended up on his knees for about thirty minutes. He received the baptism of fire and it launched him off onto a trajectory that took him to Kansas City after his release from the prison. God not only put the fire into him, but also gave him a desire to serve the Lord in foreign missions. The second brother, Richard, was a former Missionary Aviation Pilot in Africa, and was now residing in Scotland after retiring as a commercial airline pilot.

Due to problems in getting his visa into the Congo approved, brother Richard was unable to join us for the first leg of the journey into Kenya, the meeting with the students. Ronnie and I went ahead and met with the students for meetings at Kabarak University, and then for a church service in the university auditorium where we had held the kesha the previous year. It was an awesome service, a time of crying out to the Lord, of wild dancing and praise and worship. The tears of the previous year had dried, and though the scars were still there from the wounding, it was for the most part a time of rejoicing and victory.

Our walk with the Lord had given us hope, the hope that does not disappoint, and it was a blessing to be able to come back and worship with many of the same people who had been there the year before. By the end of the service, however, we were all down on our knees crying out to the Lord, and more tears fell to the ground as we prayed for protection for the mission and for the people of Kenya, to deliver them from the plans and strongholds of the enemy. After the service, a large group of us went to the local fish and chips fast food restaurant, to celebrate the victories in the spirit that comes with prayer, and praise and worship.

After an afternoon of light hearted conversation and strolling through Uhuru Park, the same park where I had been part of the All Church Picnic five years earlier, Ronnie and I began to set our sights on Mumias, where we would meet up with Pastor Lucas before the Malaba Crusade. After flying to Kisumu on Tuesday of the next week, we were met by Pastor Luke and two brothers from his church. When Ronnie and I piled into the car, we were strengthened by the fresh air and beauty surrounding Lake Victoria, one of the largest fresh water lakes of the world, as we headed north out of Kisumu for the two hour trip to Mumias. It was a great feeling to get out of the smoke and dirt of Nairobi and into some fresh air of west Kenya, to see the farmers in the fields, the small towns and villages along the highway.

We stopped at the Equator on the way north. It was a beautiful, sunny day, and we took some pictures with Ronnie and I standing alongside the road in front of a globe of the earth with the equator running around the globe. As we went on north towards Mumias, everything seemed to be going well until we got within about twenty kilometers of Mumias, where we encountered a police checkpoint, complete with spiked straps that were stretched out across the road.

It was unmistaken that there would be no passage without dealing with the police. Ostensibly, the checkpoints were established for the purpose of the looking for Al Shabaab (Somali) terrorists, weapons, and articles of warfare that could be used for acts of terror.

Unfortunately, the checkpoints have become a place for the police to extract money from people for tiny infractions of minute regulations, so they have become the face of corruption to many of the people of Kenya. The police looked at all our documents, the documents were all in order, but our car didn't have a working fire extinguisher, so we were told to sit until the officer came back to deal with us, which really meant he was coming back to get some money from us.

In the meantime, the police went about their business stopping other people as they approached the checkpoint, and while we were sitting there for over an hour, about ten vehicles of different sizes and descriptions were stopped along the road, some for just a few minutes and others for thirty minutes or longer. Even some matutus (minibuses) were being held up, and eventually the roadside was alive with people walking around, stretching their legs on the hot September day. It was very frustrating to say the least, and every time an officer walked by our car, he pretended like he had much more pressing issues to take care of than to deal with us.

I envied the bicycle and motorcycle riders who went by and were never stopped, they just breezed on by the checkpoint and on down the road. Eventually after an hour wait, the officer who had detained us came back and said for us to follow him into Mumias, the nearest city in which there was some type of a judge and traffic court. So we went around the spike strips laid out on the road and followed the officer as he headed for town. He was driving about twenty kilometers per hour, inching his way down the highway, when all of a sudden he pulled over and wanted us to pull over behind him.

But my driver had other ideas, he apparently felt like the policeman had gotten distracted by another officer where he left the road, so our driver decided to make a break for it and head on for Mumias. It was a bold move, and as a guest from a foreign country, I had no idea if he was doing the right thing, or if I was going to be spending the night in the Mumias jail! Thank God our driver knew what he was doing, as we sailed on into Mumias a few minutes later without any pursuit from the officer or other interruptions.

I was very upset about all this and wanted to go down to the police station and register a complaint about the police behavior, but Pastor Luke and the others in the car convinced me that I should just take it with a grain of salt, as he said, "that is just Kenya today." But I see in these actions the police gradually terrorizing and tormenting the people of Kenya, and so in essence the Muslim terrorists are winning, because they have caused the whole country to come under the grip of fear. It was an ominous start to the Malaba Crusade, and there would be more setbacks in the days to come, as the devil did not want me showing up in Malaba.

After stopping in Mumias to get a few food items and strolling around the open air market, we headed back out onto the highway for the trip to Pastor Luke's home and farm. His farm is located near a small village about twenty kilometers north and east of Mumias, in a rural farming area that is typical of much of the land of western Kenya. The land is very productive, gets abundant rainfall, and because of the tropical weather just about every crop known to man is easily grown and accessible there.

Fields of maize (corn), different types of beans, potatoes, sweet potatoes, tomatoes, melons, and many types of greens such as collards, spinach, and kale, were seen in abundance. The fruit and tree crops were also in abundance; oranges, lemons, avocados, mangoes, as well as some of the world's sweetest pineapples can be purchased from roadside vendors as well as the main markets in town. It is truly a buffet of fresh food! Add all that to the local chicken or goat meat, fish from Lake Victoria, and occasionally beef from the local herds, and you have a diet of fresh, tasty food, much fresher and better tasting than anything I was used to back in America.

Pastor Luke's farm is a six acre farm, surrounded by trees and others farms of similar makeup that is typical of what one sees in many areas of Africa. All the farms are worked on a daily basis, mostly by women who are out in the fields, but the fields are always populated, from early morning till late evening. Even after a rain, because of the nature of the soil, people are out in the fields the very next day, turning the ground with hand hoes or mattocks, or in some cases walking behind a couple of oxen and a single beam turning plow. It is a beautiful sight to see, especially for me coming from Kansas, where seldom are seen people actually doing hand work in the fields. It can be said of Africa, there are few machines and many people, but in America there are few people but many big machines. As we settled into our rooms at the farm, for me it felt like home, sweet home, as this was the third year that I had visited the farm, and it was to me a place of solace and refuge from the warfare and intensity of the crusades.

At the farm we were greeted warmly by all those who lived there; Mary, Pastor Luke's wife, Luke's brother and family who lived in another house on the farm, as well as his mother and sister who live in yet another house. So the whole farm is like a small village in itself, with a few head of cattle and many chickens milling around, maybe even a goat or two, quite a few children playing or working beside their parents in the field, and gardens and fruit trees everywhere there   was an inch to spare. Then on south of the Pastor's home is a larger three acre field that was the main tract for planting corn, beans, or sugarcane.

It is truly a menagerie of life that was so comforting and relaxing to be around, and as we sat down to our supper that evening, many people, from the young children to the oldest there , were present to eat with us and bless us upon arrival. As Luke prayed for the food and welcomed us, he motioned towards all the people in the room and said, "This is Africa, this is how we like it here, with many generations living together, loving and supporting one another." I had to admit I was in agreement with them, that the way they live is superior to the way many in America live, so isolated from each other in their own homes and cars.

Two days of rest at the farm did wonders to rejuvenate us and get us ready for Malaba. So on Thursday we headed to Malaba, a two hour trip to the north and west of Mumias. Malaba sits right on the Kenya-Uganda border, and there are several thousand people on each side of the border.

However, the most striking and predominate feature of the town is a continuous lineup of semi-trailer trucks; they snake their way from the border checkpoint clear back to the outskirts of town over a mile away. The line moves up slowly to the checkpoint, but because new trucks are continuously arriving from Nairobi and Mombasa on the coast of Kenya, the line never goes away. So the smell of diesel fumes, the noise of the trucks as they are inching up in the line, and the blockage of traffic exiting and entering the highway that goes through Malaba is the central feature of the town.

The checkpoint has become increasingly tedious in the last few years, as a result of terrorist attacks in Kenya and Uganda. Because those two countries are on the forefront of the thrust into Somalia to root out Al Shabaab Islamic terrorists, the reprisals against those two countries by Al Shabaab have been persistent and deadly. The Westgate Mall attack in Nairobi in the fall of 2013 was just the most visible example. Most of the trucks lined up in Malaba come from Mombasa, Kenya, a terrorist stronghold because of the high Muslim population, and most all the drivers of the trucks are Muslim. The fear by the border authorities is that the trucks are being used by terrorists to transport weapons and ammunition into central African countries of Uganda, Congo, and Central African Republic, where terrorists and rebel armies are all very active.

In addition to the lineup of trucks, there was a thriving city of businesses that had sprouted up to take care of the trucker's needs. Because the checkpoint closed down at sundown each night, there was a need for hotels, restaurants, grocery stores, electronics shops, diesel engine and tire repair, and a host of other services that lived off the presence of the trucks. As we pulled in to the city and made our way to the Harvest Church of Pastors Isaac and

Ellen, I was amazed at the sight of it all; to me it was just typical Africa, a surprise around every corner. Little did I know that I would be preaching to the truck drivers in the days ahead, as the crusade grounds were right on the main highway behind the line of trucks.

We were greeted warmly by Pastor Ellen and the elders of the church, and she informed us that Pastor Isaac would not be coming as he was in the Pennsylvania in the United States, on a mission of his own to preach in churches in America. So we all sat down to a meal of ugali, greens, chicken soup, and some great chapatis, all washed down with Fanta orange soda or Coca-Cola. By this time we were a full team, as brother Richard from Scotland had finally gotten his visa issues into the Congo straightened out, and he was able to join us for the remainder of the tour. He was certainly a blessing as he was a great Bible teacher, and when we got to the Congo we found he was an added asset in that he was fluent in French, which is the national language of the Congolese.

That afternoon at three we were going to test run the crusade by setting up the sound system and checking everything out, and a Pastor David from southern Kenya was going to bring a message to get the crowd excited and anticipating the crusade. The crusade ground was down the highway about a half mile from the church; it was about two acres, surrounded by trees and shops on two sides, then at the lower end was the platform with a huge orange and white banner across the top. The banner proclaimed in big blue letters, "MALABA MIRACLE HARVEST CHURCH BIG CRUSADE," and as I looked at that banner I thought, "Hey, that is bold, that is great!" The upper end of the ground was hemmed in by the ever present line of trucks, sitting still or creeping along on the highway, so I could quickly see that preaching to the truck drivers was going to be part of the daily routine.

The sound technicians from the church finally got the sound system up and going, after patching in a few cables and speakers, and the worship team, led by Pastor Ellen was beginning to get things going with some good praise and worship and dancing to the Lord. Many of those dancing around on the grass in front of the platform were children from the church and the city; they really enjoy the music and love to be in the proximity to the crusade. Some of the children were also orphans, and so they hope by being around the crusade, someone will feed or care for them, or maybe even take them in and give them a place to live. So everyone was having a high time praising the Lord, and few paid much notice to the ominous storm clouds that were starting to gather overhead, until eventually the beautiful, sunny day was gone, and gray and black, angry looking clouds took their place.

I was standing back near the highway watching everything take place, when suddenly, about twenty feet in front of me, I saw a twelve foot high speaker stand start to blow over by a violent gust of wind.

The speaker on top of the stand was a heavy, outdoor public address speaker about four feet tall, and the stand itself was heavy, welded together out of square tubing, so the whole apparatus weighed hundreds of pounds. I saw Pastor Luke was right in the path of the speaker as it blew over, so I screamed at him at the top of my lungs, "Look out!," just as the speaker came crashing down on his head. He never had a chance to even see what hit him, as it buckled his knees and knocked him several feet forward, but didn't knock him to the ground. By the time I had come rushing up to his side to help hold him up, I could see a big gash on the top of his head that was bleeding profusely, so I pulled a napkin out of my back pocket and applied it with pressure to his head.

Pastor Luke was stunned and dazed, and for my part I was more worried about him having a broken neck or a fractured skull, and so I asked him, "Are you okay?'. He mumbled a reply, "Yes, brother, I will be okay, just keep everything going!" By that time Luke's wife and some others had gathered around to help hold him up, and they decided to immediately take him off to look for a clinic, as they feared for the worst as I did. So off they went, weaving their way through the line of trucks, and as God would have it, there was a clinic right across the street from the crusade ground, complete with a doctor and nurse on call, so that is where they ended up. After about an hour I went over to check on them, and they were in line to get attention, and Pastor Luke's wife was holding a thumb's up to me as if to say, "We have everything under control, no need for you to stay around."

I went back over to the crusade where Pastor David was beginning to get fired up and preach a powerful message, and the storm was also getting fired up with lots of gusty wind, even some sprinkles and light showers. But David was undaunted, and as the worship team came up for the altar call, several people came forward to accept the Lord Jesus as their personal Savior. About that time Pastor Luke showed up after his visit to the clinic. He had blood on his shirt and a big white patch that really stood out on top of his black head, but other than that seemed to be in pretty good shape, with no major injuries to report. I asked him, "How are you doing?" He replied "I'm doing good brother, what the devil meant for harm the Lord is going to turn around for His good." We both got a good laugh out of that, as I told him from my vantage point it looked like it was going to be an extremely serious injury. Again, he repeated, "it's just a little sore, but I'm going to be okay," so we both praised God for sparing him any worse fate.

Needless to say, the sound technicians moved the speaker stand up next to the platform and lashed it with ropes to the platform, and we never had any more problems with that the rest of the week. But as I was thinking back over the events of the day, I was reminded of the Scripture where Jesus spoke to the disciples concerning John the Baptist, *"And from the days of John the Baptist until now the kingdom of heaven suffers violence, and the violent take it by force."* (Matthew 11:12) What he meant was that we have to press in with perseverance and take the territory back from the enemy by tenacity, and sometimes it involves violent warfare when the enemy is out to destroy the kingdom of God. The whole day to me seemed like a microcosm of that battle; the enemy was doing everything possible to slow down and discourage the warriors of God from going forward, it looked like the opening salvo in a battle that was going to rage for the next few days.

The next day the crusade schedule began in earnest, with a pastor training session beginning at ten each morning, then the crusade in the afternoon at four. The pastor training sessions were led by Pastor Ellen and the worship team, and I'd have to say I have never seen such exuberant praise and dancing before the Lord in all my years in Africa. Ellen is an extremely anointed worship leader, the praise just comes boiling up out of every pore of her body, soul, and spirit, and it is infectious to anyone who happens to be in close proximity. As she and the team got going, long lines of people danced though the aisles of the church led by the forward guard of people waving gold, blue, and purple banners.

It was a beautiful sight to see the freedom enjoyed by these precious children of God, and I am always amazed by the joy and freedom of the people in Africa, who despite their lack of material blessings that we in America would consider essential, have such joy in their lives. It is truly an inspiration to see them worship, the Psalmist had it right when he said, *"Praise the Lord! For it is good to sing praises to our God; for it is pleasant, and praise is beautiful."* (Psalm 147:1)

The teaching sessions of the pastor training were great as well, with Ronnie, Richard, and Pastor David all taking a turn sharing messages and teachings. Brother Ronnie gave a testimony of how he had been in prison in America, and the Lord had used that time to humble him and draw him back to the faith given to him in his childhood. He told about how he first started getting in trouble with the law, he was arrested at age fourteen for aggravated assault and selling of drugs. He went from a detention facility to a Christian academy in Georgia and thought he was getting his life back on track, only to find out the devil had other plans for him. Within a couple of years after graduating from the academy, he was back into addiction and selling of drugs, even to the point of running major supplies of drugs from one state to another. While on a run to Kansas City, he was stopped and searched and arrested for possession and sale of drugs, and he ended up in a state prison where I met him at a Friday night prison callout.

His story takes an amazing turn from there, as one Friday night during a worship session, the Holy Spirit fire hit him and put him down on his knees for thirty minutes, and he received that baptism of fire that John the Baptist said would come with the coming of Jesus Christ. John the Baptist spoke about it when he said, *"I indeed baptize you with water for repentance, but He who is coming after me is mightier that I, whose sandals I am not worthy to carry. He will baptize you with the Holy Spirit and with fire!"* (Matthew 3:11)

And so after that night Ronnie's life took on a whole new meaning, and he became "on fire" for the Lord, and when he got released from prison he started looking for doors of opportunity where he could serve the kingdom of God. That search took him to Kansas City and into Bible studies and a steady walk with the Lord at one of the great churches in Kansas City, and from there to Africa to travel with me for the duration of the mission trip.

Brother Richard's story is equally as compelling, though he didn't take the detour through the prison and detention facility. In fact, he received a Bible college degree, and became a trained pilot, with his first kingdom service was as a pilot for MAF, Mission Aviation Fellowship, a mission organization that operates all over the globe.

Their primary mission is to ferry supplies and missionaries into hard to reach areas, the backwoods outposts of Africa or Asia where lack of roads make it practically impossible to reach the lost for the kingdom. After flying missions into Chad and other African countries for eight years, he took his aviator skills to the commercial market and became a pilot for a commercial airline near his home base of Scotland. His gospel fire was burning bright throughout the tour, and his ability to bring keen insight into the life of Jesus and the stories of the Bible made him an instant hit with the other pastors and teachers.

The afternoon crusade started as it did the day before, under a blue sky with a promising crowd starting to gather. As the worship team began to sing and dance, many children started to gather, as well as people from the churches of the area, and some bystanders and strangers off the street. And of course, the ever present truck drivers who were taking it all in, enjoying the relief from the tedium of waiting in line for the trucks to move up to the border checkpoint. The children especially were having a great time; one of the dances they do is a circle dance where they follow the leader and mimic his gyrations, all the while waving branches of leaves they have broken off the nearby bushes and trees. The purpose of the dance is to memorialize the joyful time when Jesus triumphantly came riding into Jerusalem on a donkey, so they wave the branches back and forth in front of themselves as they go dancing , twirling, skipping and hopping about in a long chain of bodies.

As the worship team began to sing from up on the platform, again few people were noticing the dark clouds that were rolling in, and it started to look like a remake of yesterday. By the time I got up to preach, the winds were starting to gust, the trees and bushes were beginning to shake violently, and it looked as if the banner over the platform was going to blow away. Then about that time it settled down somewhat and just became a good, soaking rainstorm, so much so that everyone out in the gathering sought shelter from the downpour, and it was just myself and the interpreter standing up there all alone.

I was totally soaked by the time they got an umbrella to us, so I continued to preach to an audience of one, that being brother Ronnie who stood out in the rain listening till the end, from what had shortly before been a few hundred people. It all looked rather hilarious from my point of view, and I'm sure Jesus got a good laugh out of it as well!

After a downpour of about thirty minutes, the rain started to let up, and by the time I got around to giving the altar call about sundown, a handful of people had drifted back onto the crusade grounds from the neighboring businesses and shelters where they had run. One lone person came forward to accept to accept Jesus, and another man gave a testimony about how he had stopped at the crusade on his way to the clinic to have his eye looked at, he was suffering from severe pain in his eye that was causing him a lot of grief. Just being there at the crusade the Lord had given him relief from the eye pain, so he was happy to share the news about the healing with the others in attendance. The whole afternoon again seemed like it was tough going, through the storm and then with only one person making a decision, but after many years of preaching I have learned to accept the will of God in these situations, God knows the hearts of the people there and their reasons for being there.

The next two days were much better weather wise; we had sunny skies and very little wind. I got up and preached with all my heart the two days, many people came forward for prayers for healing and to rededicate their lives, but the total of first time salvation decisions was probably less than fifteen total. I was perplexed and wondering why we put all that effort and expenditure into such a small harvest, and wondering if there was something I needed to hear from the Lord or do differently. After the final meeting on Sunday night, we went back to the hotel, and three or four of us went next door to the restaurant to get a bite to eat and talk over the events of the weekend.

We were all in agreement that the plowing had been pretty slow going, I could certainly relate to the analogy Jesus used about the parable of the sower, where He declared, *"A sower went out to sow, and as he sowed, some seed fell by the wayside; and the birds came and devoured them."* (Matthew 13:4) Then He went on later in that parable and gave an interpretation, by saying, *"When anyone hears the word of the kingdom, and does not understand it, then the wicked one comes and snatches away what was sown in his heart. This is he who received seed by the wayside."* (Matthew 13:19) As I was sharing my feelings with Pastor Luke, he encouraged me greatly when he said,

"Brother, just about all these people around here are Muslims, and the ones who came forward to receive salvation are Muslims as well." I replied, "Well, that certainly explains why the plowing has been so difficult in this place!," and I felt a whole lot better about the results.

We dived into our plates of chicken and chips, and just about the time we were finishing up, two children who had been at the crusade, a young boy about eight and a girl about ten, came up and stood beside our table. They had very forlorn and empty looks on their faces. Richard and Ronnie chipped in and ordered some chicken and chips for them, which was ready and given to them in just a few minutes. As they exited the restaurant, Brother Luke said to me, "Those children are orphan children, and that is why they were in the restaurant begging food, they looked very hungry. They come to the crusades, hoping someone will look out for them and feed them."

My heart broke for those children as I thought about all those in Kenya and Africa who had no home, and empty stomachs when they laid down to sleep. I prayed to the Lord to bless the children, and vowed that if I could do something to help them I would. I was going to get wholeheartedly behind Pastor Luke's desire to build an orphanage near his farm at Mumias, to be a conduit for resources flowing from America to the poor in Kenya.

The pastor training and encouragement sessions at the Harvest Church had been extraordinarily good, with a large contingent of pastors from Uganda coming over to receive the blessing of the good teachings. Pastor Ellen was magnificent in leading praise and worship each day, and on Sunday morning a powerful healing and anointing wind of the Holy Spirit blew through the service when Pastor David was preaching. David was breathing fire, exhorting the people of the church, and he took on the mantle of David the shepherd boy when he slayed Goliath the giant. He called all the worship teams and leaders forward who were there in church that morning, and as they linked arms he blew the fresh breath of the Holy Spirit on them all, and the power of God went through them like a tsunami! It was an awesome sight to see God move so powerfully. Then David called me up to speak over the men of the church, and I prayed over them and anointed them with fresh fire, then I turned around and laid hands on David and blessed him with fresh fire, and the anointing for creative miracles. It was an awesome service and a powerful way to end the week.

Monday is often pastors rest day as most pastors work day is on Sunday, and so Monday we were certainly all in a mood to take it easy and rest on our laurels. We were going to be leaving Malaba about ten in the morning heading back to Mumias, and after meeting at the restaurant to have some good Kenya tea and milk, we all mused about the events of the week. "Who knows, maybe our greatest victories were in preaching the word to all the Muslim truck drivers who were sitting in line on the highway!" I said, as we all spoke our goodbyes and prepared to leave. "Only God knows for sure, and we'll find out when we get to heaven."

CHAPTER 17
Goma, DROC 2014

Since our trip to Goma in the Democratic Republic of Congo in 2012, many things had happened in Goma that had reinforced my belief that God wanted us to go back again. After a period of instability immediately after we left, the rebels had gone back out into the country and there had been a peace agreement forged between them and the Congolese government in Kinshasha. They had been convinced to lay down their arms, and international attention and pressure had forced them to somewhat abandon the push to take over North Kivu State, where there had been so much turmoil and chaos the preceding thirty years. From my vantage point in America, and reinforced by the Congolese Pastor Isaiah, who had made several trips back to Goma in the ensuing years, it did appear that a time of relative peace and stability may be settling in on the Congo.

Pastor Isaiah had been in touch with Pastor Joseph of the church in Goma where I had preached on Sunday morning of the crusade, and he and a group of pastors were anxious for me to come back. So we made plans to go back to Goma, and I have to say I was very excited to be going back; I wanted to see what the Lord had done in the two years since we were there and spoke the prophetic message of King Jehoshaphat over that region. And the second reason was just the challenge of the new frontier; the Congo is so deep into the heart of Africa and a place where many fear to tread, so I just get a sense of a rush of excitement whenever I think about it. It is the same rush as thinking about scaling a high mountain, or kayaking down a wild river, or for myself going into those places where the outcasts dwell.

Ronnie and I had applied for our Congolese visas back in the states, and outside of getting a yellow fever shot prior to submitting the application, there were no major issues, and both of us had our passports back to us and stamped within four or five days. Brother Richard over in Scotland had a different story; however, after paying an intermediary to file the necessary paperwork for him, it still took him over a month to receive his visa, and caused him to miss the first part of the mission, the student meetings in Nairobi. But all of that was behind us now as we flew from Kisumu back to Nairobi, then rested up in a hotel to prepare for the flight to Kigali, Rwanda, which would take us within a four hour bus trip to our destination of Goma.

I had been given several prophetic words before I left Kansas regarding the trip to Africa; one in particular was profound and caused me to brace myself spiritually for the trip. A Prophetess named Jane, from the east coast, who has been a regular fixture in my life since about 2008 when she contacted me for the first time, and prophesied over me that I would be going to the nations of the world to preach the gospel, called a couple of weeks before my departure date. She didn't know that I was going to be leaving for Africa again, she just said, "The Holy Spirit told me to call you." I was grateful for her call, and listened intently as she began to speak.

She said, "The Lord is saying, 'You are going to a new level of spiritual warfare, a place that you have never been before." And she exhorted me with these words, "Do not shrink back in fear. Fear God, but do not fear man. Many around you will be speaking fear over you, but do not receive it." Then she spoke a couple of Scriptures over me, the first in Hebrews, in which the Apostle Paul encouraged the Hebrews to stand firm in the battle. The Scripture states, *"You have not yet resisted to bloodshed, in your striving against sin".* (Hebrews 12:4) When she spoke that, I had a little gut check and knew instantly she was prophesying about the Congo, as the warfare there is especially intense due to all the chaos and mayhem that has been going on there for so many years. Any time a person sees that type of demonic activity in the natural, you can be assured the devil wants to keep his hold on the earthly realm, and so the spiritual battle in those regions is especially intense.

In addition to the spiritual battle, the fear factor is also constantly an issue regarding the Congo. Many people equate the destruction and chaos in the Congo as the common face of Africa, and so they speak that over a person when the subject comes up. I had to admit, at times I, too, let fear grip me, but each time it tried to creep in, I just spent time in prayer about the situation and turned it over to the Lord. I'm learning in my kingdom walk, that the safest place to be is in the center of God's will, and it isn't necessarily associated with any geographical location, whether in Africa or anywhere else.

She talked about Jesus shedding His precious blood for us as well, "in His battle against sin, He was even shedding blood for us in the garden when He was praying for us, about taking up the cup of suffering and interceding for us on the cross." And when I thought about it, her word had really nailed me, I hadn't really ever shed much blood in my battle against sin, and I can truthfully say I wasn't especially looking forward to doing that, but I'm sure Jesus didn't either. In spite of the many travels and the years of preaching, the Lord had preserved me and protected everywhere I went, and outside of some cuts and scratches on my hands while building houses in Juarez, I can't say that I've left any measurable blood behind.

The second Scripture she spoke over me was from the famous passage about our warfare battle that the Apostle Paul gave to the baby Christians at Ephesus. He told them, "For we do not wrestle against flesh and blood, but against principalities, against powers, against the rulers of the darkness of this age, against spiritual hosts of wickedness in the heavenly places." Then Paul went on to explain, *"Therefore, take up the whole armor of God, that you may be able to withstand in the evil day, and having done all, to stand"* (Ephesians 6:12,13) She said, "This is most certainly the evil day, and the Lord will fight the battles and protect you as you come against the enemy. High level spiritual warfare is not pretty! The whole earth is encountering a level of spiritual warfare that it has never known before; this is the sign of the last days." So I had been given this word and after the trip was over I realized it was for not only the Congo, but aptly applied to a lesser degree to the crusade in Malaba as well.

Another prophecy that was spoken over me had to do with the trip from Kigali, Rwanda, to Goma, and also about the actual crusade in Goma. A prayer brother began speaking over me as I related the details of the trip to him, especially regarding the last leg of the journey to the Congo. He said, "The Lord is going to translate you from Kigali to Goma, just as he did with Phillip after he had baptized the Ethiopian eunuch." And I thought to myself, "Well now, that's going to be interesting!" Then the brother spoke about the actual crusade, "That angels and

Jesus Himself would manifest themselves at the crusade, and that at times as I am preaching, the anointing of the Holy Spirit will be so strong on me, I would have a difficult time standing up." As he spoke those words, I came to a place of great anticipation and expectation for the time in the Congo, and felt in my spirit that it was going to be a very special time.

All those thoughts were floating around in my mind as we flew from Kisumu, on the shore of Lake Victoria in farthest west Kenya, back to Nairobi. We were scheduled to get a hotel room in Nairobi that Monday night, then early the next morning be back at the airport to board for the two hour flight to Kigali, then on to Goma. Our connection in Nairobi, who booked the hotel for us and who was to pick us up at the airport and take us to the hotel, was Larry, the younger brother of Pastor Luke from Mumias. He had grown up out on the farm near Mumias, but as many Kenyans of the last generation have done, migrated to Nairobi seeking his livelihood; the prospects of farming a small patch of ground out in rural Kenya just did not appeal to him. I had met him before this one time, he came to the Mumias crusade in 2011, so I was confident he would have a good place for us in Nairobi, and would deliver us there safe and sound.

We greeted each other warmly when we met after the flight, and after introducing brothers Ronnie and Richard to him, we all piled into his car for the "twenty minute" ride to the hotel. The twenty minute ride is a bit of an inside joke the people of Nairobi play on foreign visitors who have never sat in the "jam," the monster traffic jams that plague Nairobi day and night. A highway infrastructure that was built for 1970 traffic load, is still trying to move the overflow of vehicles that are used in the bustling city of over four million people.

So it is not unusual to sit in the jam for an hour or more, sometimes two hours, waiting to get to your destination. However, whenever a foreigner asks a Kenyan driver how far away a place is, or how long it will take to get there, the standard answer is always "about twenty minutes!" After a few trips across Nairobi over the years that I have been there, I just begin to go with the flow and say, "This is just Nairobi, it is the price to pay for coming to Africa for Jesus!"

Larry's driver had us all entertained for a bit, talking nonstop about all the corruption in Kenya, and who all had made off with the people's money, and what they had subsequently done with it. But after the first "twenty minutes" his stories were starting to get a bit boring. We were all anxious to get to the hotel, where we could get a good meal and rest up for the next day's journey, which would begin at five in the morning, to leave the hotel headed for the airport. So when we began bouncing around on a terribly rocky and rutted out road on the outskirts of Nairobi, we were all beginning to wonder what was up, so I questioned brother Larry, "Where in the world is this hotel you said was only twenty minutes from the airport?" With a big grin on his face, he replied, "Oh, it's up the way a bit, we're going to take you over to Pastor Matthew's church in Embakasi, he wants to greet you before you take off for the Congo."

Had I not known brother Larry and Pastor Matthew, the same pastor who had ministered with us at the Mumias Crusade, and then again over in Tororo, I probably would have jumped out of the car at that point, I was feeling a bit like I had been kidnapped. But we all had a good laugh over the detour, though after bouncing around on the rough road for over an hour, we were certainly ready to be at our destination, whether Matthew's church, or to the hotel.

Just when our patience was about to give out, we pulled up in front of a sheet metal structure, a church plant in the midst of thousands of residential apartment dwellings, and Pastor Matthew came bounding out of the church to greet us. It was very good to see him and renew our ties; I had come to really enjoy his preaching and friendship when we were together the previous two years.

Matthew invited us into his office for some hot tea and rolls, and he had a good visit getting to know my comrades, Ronnie and Richard. And just as we were about ready to wind up the conversation Matthew announced. "We're having a service at six-thirty tonight for the elders and leaders of his church, and we'd like for you guys to stay and speak to them." We all agreed to do that, but only on the condition that it would be brief, as we all felt the need to rest up before the trip tomorrow. So the kidnapping was really a plot to get us to speak to his church people, and by six-thirty that evening, people began to show up and waited for us to speak. Each of the three of us spoke for about ten minutes; we thanked them for the invitation to stay longer, but asked to be excused so we could go to the hotel and rest up, which they kindly allowed us to do. In parting, I spoke to the people, "Pray for us earnestly that the Lord would protect us, and move in a mighty way over in Goma." And after they all prayed a blessing over us, we departed for the hotel, knowing the detour was of the Lord, so we could receive the extra blessings.

In the morning we were up and out of bed at four-thirty sharp, loaded into Larry's car, on our way to the airport by five. Because of the time of the day, the "twenty minute" drive this time only took an hour, though fifteen minutes of the trip we spent waiting for one of the kesha students to show up at a street corner with a pair of my shoes, which I had left in his apartment on the first week of the tour. But that went off as planned, and we arrived at the airport by six, where we were met by Pastor Isaiah, the native Congolese now living in Nairobi, who was going to accompany us to Goma. Many of his family still live in the Congo, in a city two hours north of Goma, including his brother who is the owner of the family brick making business. So we were now a team of four, and we made it through all the checkpoints and boarded a Kenya Airways flight for Kigali at eight that morning. As we flew towards Kigali, I was anxiously anticipating the next leg of the journey, when we would be met at the airport by some of the brothers from Goma, who were responsible for taking us the rest of the way to the Congo.

We were met by three brothers from Pastor Joseph's church from Goma, and after introductions, we all jumped into a minibus and took off, first though the refreshingly clean streets and highways of Kigali, then on out onto the open road that winds from Kigali to Goma. When we traveled on that road in 2012, there were five of us plus the driver shoehorned into a little car that was small for four people, and the trip was extremely uncomfortable to say the least. I didn't get to enjoy the beauty of the countryside because I was being squeezed to death by a door on one side and a much bigger pastor on the other.

But this trip was much different; we all had plenty of room to stretch out in the minivan, even slide side to side to take pictures and truly enjoy the scenery of the Rwandan countryside. The farms were so immaculate and well-tended, just like the streets of Kigali, and the mosaic of crops in the valleys and terraced hillsides, for this farmer from Kansas it was an inspiring sight to behold.

Many people were out in the fields, planting potatoes, pole beans or corn, and others were harvesting sugar cane, collards or sweet potatoes. Some of the higher elevation valleys and hillsides were covered with brilliant green tea bushes, and all the little village shops along the way had famous Rwandan tea for sale. Midway through the journey we stopped at a small roadside mountain village, and we all bought some samosas, small bierock -type, filled pastries and sodas, to nourish us for the last half of the journey. As we wound around on the highway making our way towards Goma, we began to descend from the high elevations and go downhill, our Congolese Pastor Isaiah shouted out, "Goma, my city, here we come!" He was so excited to be going home it just about caused him to burst.

As we approached Gisenyi, Rwanda, the last city in Rwanda that we would exit from into Congo, I thought about the trip from Kigali and how pleasant and truly joyful it had been compared to 2012, and then the Holy Spirit spoke to me about the prophesy of being translated to Goma. I had to agree I felt like we had just been translated, it was that smooth, though not quite in the same spiritual vein as Phillip was in the book of Acts. But I was certainly enjoying it just the same!

As we entered through the port of entry into Goma, we passed under a large green sign, stretched across the highway that read: "Welcome to the Democratic Republic of Congo." My heart skipped a beat as we went through all the checkpoints, displayed our yellow fever vaccination certificates and visas to the authorities. I was beginning to feel the anxiety and excitement of the crusades from when we were here last in 2012. There was virtually no one ahead of us in the visa lines, few people were lining up to go into the Congo, it was obvious that this part of the Congo was still perceived, for the most part, as being too hot to handle. The reputation of North Kivu State, and of Goma for being ground zero for all the chaos and rebel activity, was going to be a difficult reputation to live down. But the anticipation of the new and what was yet to come quickly overcame any anxiety I had from the past.

We were met by Pastor Joseph, his wife, and a host of other brothers from his Deliverance Church, and after introductions all the way around, we made our way across the rocky volcanic streets of Goma. The best thing to say about the volcanic rock streets is that they never get muddy, but because they are molten lava that came from Mt. Nyiragongo a few kilometers to the north, they never get smooth either. So every trip to the hotel or the church was a jostling affair, by the time we got to wherever we were going, it felt like we had been rocks shaken around in an aluminum can. The entourage of cars carrying us and the pastors finally made its way to the Cap Kivu Hotel, a beautiful bed and breakfast hotel on the shore of Lake Kivu. As we entered the hotel and were appointed our rooms, I was a bit astounded by the luxury and beauty of the place; it was way above anything I had seen in 2012 when visiting Goma.

We were directed up the stairs by a hotel assistant, and entered what turned out to be the room the pastors had reserved for me. The pastors were very proud of the accommodations, and they were all smiles as they paced around the room, showing off the bed, and then into the bathroom, showing off the beautifully tiled facilities. Then we all went out onto the balcony, where a stunning view of Lake Kivu and the surrounding mountains was on display. But in spite of their obvious pride in the facility for us, the main thought that was going through my mind was, "How in the world are we going to pay for this place?" I had told my traveling mates to budget for a sixty dollar a night hotel in Goma, thinking that would be way above and beyond anything that we would need. And after spending a week in Malaba at a decent ten dollar a night place, I couldn't see how we could possibly justify this several star place, and after glancing at Ronnie and Richard, I knew they were thinking the same thing.

So I decided to do the embarrassing thing and talk it out with Pastor Joseph. I took him and my traveling mates out onto the balcony where we had a meeting of the minds on the lavish rooms appointed for us. I dived into the touchy conversation this way, "Pastor, we do not expect this type of accommodation, it is way more than we need, we are here to share the gospel, this isn't what we need. Just how much are the rooms here anyway?" He replied, "The rooms are one hundred twenty five dollars per night, but we got a special rate for you visitors of only eighty per night, and the breakfasts are free!"

In addition to that, he made the most important point, "This is where the President of the Congo stays when he comes to Goma, and we want you to have the very best!" So I answered back to him, "We thank you for thinking so highly of us to provide the very best, but this is way over our budget to even think of staying in such a place." Inwardly I was thinking, "That price isn't too bad for all the luxury, it would be at least double that in America."

At that point I thought we had severely offended them, but I was prepared to pick up our bags and go look for something a bit less ostentatious. About that time Pastor Joseph had a small conference with his other pastors, and then he came back out onto the balcony where we were gathered to make his final declaration. He said, "We have saved in the church for a year and a half to provide the very best for you, and we want you to stay here. So we will pick up the hotel tab for all four of you, all you have to do is ask for Ronnie and Richard to pay their own meal tickets, and we will call that good, if you guys would be satisfied with that." I looked at Ronnie and Richard, and both nodded that would be more than satisfactory, and so we settled into our rooms without offending our hosts, very thankful for the beautiful accommodations they had sacrificed to provide for us. So the pastors left, very proud of the fact they had provided for us to stay in the finest place in Goma.

The food at the Cap Kivu was just as exquisite as the rooms, though a bit pricey at fifteen to twenty dollars a plate, but the variety and quality was again beyond anything I expected to see in the Congo. Many fish and chicken entrees with a variety of vegetables, and the favorite of everyone, chips, or French fries, came with many of the entrees and were almost a meal unto itself. And, of course the breakfasts, which came free with the room, were an extravaganza of soups, breads, scrambled eggs, and a huge variety of fresh fruit. The breakfast hour also had some excitement of its own regarding three or four crested herons, large, silver colored birds with a funny looking topnotch on top of their heads. They were the pet birds of the hotel and wandered around on the grounds, at the amusement of the guests.

Since I am an early riser, most mornings I was down at the dining room, which was a covered patio overlooking the grounds and Lake Kivu, every morning by six o'clock. I like to rise early, get a good cup of hot coffee, read my Bible, and prepare for the days teaching or message in the quiet and stillness of the morning. Nearly every morning I was the lone occupant of the restaurant, save for the crested herons who would work their way up the twenty or so steps from the courtyard to the restaurant. Then they would sneak over to the buffet line, as the waiters were just bringing out the buffet entrees for the breakfast. And if the waiters were back in the kitchen, or tending to some other preparations, the birds would attempt to snatch a hot roll or piece of wheat bread, then turn and run back down the steps and out of the dining area.

If they were quick enough, they would get away with their prize, but if the waiters saw them, they would come running out of the kitchen with towels waving in the air, sending the birds scattering and back down the steps to the courtyard. Then the waiters would go back to their business, and the whole scene would play out again, over and over, until finally the waiters became angry enough to really chase the birds a long way, or the dining area began to fill up by seven, to the point the birds felt uncomfortable taking the chance to go in. It was a hilarious battle that went on every day, from six until about seven in the morning.

The first full day in Goma we were on our way over to Pastor Joel's church for a revival preparation session, when we stopped along the way at the church of a Prophetess Deborah, who was the Pastor of another church in town. They were having a meeting that afternoon, and we stopped to speak for a few minutes, mainly to invite them to the crusade and pastor training, which would begin the next day and go through the weekend. Prophetess Deborah got up to speak and welcome us to Goma and her church, and she spoke about our coming. "The Lord showed me in a dream two years ago, there would be three wazungus (white men) coming to minister to the city of Goma, and to this church." She went on to say, "You three are the fulfillment of that prophetic dream, and now we say thank you for coming, we look forward to the crusade and to hear what the Lord has to say through you for this city." We were amazed at that prophecy, and I thought about the fact that it was exactly two years ago when I was last here. The Lord certainly knew my comings and goings, and ordained them all!

After leaving the Prophetess's church, we went over to downtown Goma to visit some of the local dignitaries. We first stopped off at the office of the district police headquarters, and introduced ourselves to the officer in charge there, and thanked her for the security we would be having at the crusade. She was a Christian and was very thankful for us to be in Goma. From there we went to the Mayor's office, and we were given an audience with the Mayor, as he had told Pastor Joseph he wanted to give his blessings to the crusade before it started.

When we got into the Mayor's office, we were introduced to him, and again we were made to feel very welcome for coming to the city. He told us that he had been in exile in South America until two years ago, when the Lord told him to go back to Goma, that it was time to return to help restore and rebuild the war torn capitol city. I thought back again to the time reference of two years, the very time when we claimed the victory of King Jehoshaphat over the rebel army, and now this very brilliant man before us had been called to return.

I prophesied over him, that the Lord was going to use him in greater measure, not only as a political leader, but also in the spiritual dimension as well; that God had called him back for a very special reason, and the Mayor's job was just a stepping stone to take him higher and higher in all the kingdom realms of his life. Before we left, the Mayor got down on his knees in front of us and asked us to lay hands on him and pray for him, which we gladly did, and we were so thankful God had placed this man in the office for just a time such as this. It was going to be a great time for Goma!

After making our way over to Deliverance Church, we had a rousing meeting with many of his church people, then went back to the hotel to rest up and prepare for the next day's full slate of events. The next morning after arriving at the church at nine, we were pleased to see many pastors from the Goma area file in. Some I recognized from the time I was there in 2012, and altogether there were over seventy five in attendance. After a glorious time of praise and worship, each of us visitors were given time to speak, and I gave a teaching on the use of the anointing oil as a symbolic representation of the Holy Spirit. The pastors were very appreciative of the message, as I knew from my visit in 2012, there was much confusion on the subject in their fellowship. Some charlatans had come through Goma selling bottles of oils for one hundred dollars each, and so some of the pastors had banned the use of the oil altogether. As a result, I wanted to help them understand the beneficial use of the oil, how it symbolized the Holy Spirit, and it was not to be used by unscrupulous people just to exploit or extract money from others.

By the time the crusade started up at three in the afternoon, the skies were starting to get cloudy after a beautiful sunny morning. After an hour and a half of praise and worship by several different worship teams, all brightly dressed in their matching uniforms, the skies were looking very ominous. Within about thirty minutes after I started to speak, it began to rain, lightly at first and then a steady downpour, and again I found myself getting soaking wet preaching at a crusade. The people were getting wet, but many had come prepared and brought umbrellas, and many others ducked into the church, where they could hear me, but in many cases not see me because of the configuration of the platform to the church. I pressed on, however, undaunted by the fact that now I was pretty much soaked, though my interpreter was given an umbrella to hold over my head to at least protect me from getting any wetter, and also to preserve the microphone from any damage.

The platform was set out in the street facing the church, and the people listening were down the street to the left, to the right, and directly ahead in the street and in the church. It was a strange configuration, but the church brothers decided to do it that way, to be able to easily set up the stage with the sound system that was used every day by the church. As I gazed to my right, there was a big mountain at the head of the street, about two kilometers away up the street. And to my left, at an elevation of over eleven thousand feet, Mt. Nyiragongo, was just a few kilometers away in that direction, on the other side of Lake Kivu. But because it is such a large mountain, its hulking presence makes it feel much closer than it really is. We were a sea of humanity in between the two mountains, getting soaked by the early rain for Jesus and taking it all in.

As I gave the altar call, I kept looking back and forth between the two mountains, expecting at any moment to see angels or Jesus manifest, as I harkened back to the prophetic word spoken over me before I left Kansas. I never did see either, but I'm sure someone did, as the power of God was so strong at the altar I could barely stand.

Many came rushing forward for both salvation decisions and for prayers for healing, and as I spoke over those standing in front of the altar, their tears were mixed with the rain, and it was a great time of cleansing and deliverance for the many who came forward.

I looked again to my left to see the majestic sight of the volcanic Mt. Nyiragongo, as it spewed a never ending column of smoke and steam out the top and up into the misty clouds hanging over it. The mountain was reminding me that, yes, our God is a consuming fire! It was a great start to the week, with many making decisions for the Lord and receiving a touch of His healing power.

When we came the next day for the pastor training at nine in the morning, the church brothers had been very busy and had built an awning that completely covered the platform, as well as all the big speakers that were on the roof of the church. We were prepared for whatever would come our way, as it was forecast that rain again would move into the area by the middle of the afternoon. The pastor training was again well attended, and the worship time was up in the heavenlies, with people dancing around to the Lord just as I had remembered them dancing on the night of the Jehoshaphat praise extravaganza in 2012. I gave a teaching on "Five attributes of a good leader," and brother Ronnie and brother Richard each gave a teaching as well, and we finished up with soda and bread cakes about one in the afternoon.

Immediately after the training session ended, about ten of us jumped into vehicles and went over to the Goma prison, a facility that houses local and North Kivu State inmates. Pastor Joseph, Prophetess Deborah, her Associate Pastor, a few other brothers from the church, as well as Ronnie, Richard, and me went in. After checking all our phones and personal paraphernalia at the office of the warden, we went into the entry of the main cell block. The warden had warned us not to touch the walls of the prison so as to avoid getting lice, and we could see how easy it would be as the prison was extremely crowded and dirty beyond belief. Some of the inmate's families were visiting that day, as it was a Saturday, and they were bringing in food and clothing for their loved ones. But for the most part it was a very depressing place, beyond anything I had ever seen anywhere in the states or even in Kamiti Prison in Nairobi.

The prison had been built for two hundred inmates, and it now housed over eleven hundred; but in addition to that, we were told that the government only provided enough food for two hundred, and so many were hungry and sick, and were it not for churches and family bringing in supplies to them, they would surely starve and die. So many of the inmates sold themselves to the others for sex in exchange for food and clothing, the whole place reeked of the stronghold of the devil. It was awful! We forged ahead with a service, initiated by a couple of drummers who got a beat going, then the inmates chimed in and began to sing some praise songs, and in practically no time we had two to three hundred inmates pressed in closely around us , with no more than three feet separating us from them in every direction.

Ronnie was the first to speak, and he gave a powerful testimony of his time in prison in the United States. He told how he had first been incarcerated when he was fourteen years old, and then he went back and forth with his walk with the Lord, never quite committing himself fully to his walk. He knew what he wanted and needed to do, he just never could quite get there. But when he got arrested and put in the Kansas State Prison for two years, he knew he had to make some changes, and only the Lord could help him to make the needed changes. The Goma inmates listened intently to the message; they were captivated by this good looking young man, who they never would have suspected was coming to minister to them just a year or so after being released from prison. But Ronnie is a living testimony to the power of God to change lives.

After Ronnie spoke, I got up and gave a salvation message and invitation to the inmates to make a decision for Jesus, or to rededicate their life to serve Him and honor Him. Though we were all so cramped together there was no coming forward to the altar, many raised their hands in agreement that this was what they wanted to do with their life. I finished by leading them in a prayer of repentance, and then we made our way back out of the place, sorry to have to leave them in that wretched circumstance, but grateful for the opportunity to share the love of Jesus in that place. I was again reminded of scripture, as the writer of Hebrews exhorts, *"Remember the prisoners as if chained with them- those who are mistreated-since you yourselves are in the body also."* (Hebrews 13:3) That was certainly the case here; I believe we were more blessed than they for the time that we spent with them.

That afternoon at the crusade, we had a good crowd again, and off and on rain again. The highlight of the praise and worship time was the presence of a lady from Texas who came up on the platform to lead a time of worship. I was shocked to see someone from Texas in Goma, so I asked her husband, "What brings you people to Goma?"

He said, "My wife is a worship leader and is a native of the Congo. She and I had come back to Congo to do some recording and visit her family in Kinshasha, on the west side of the Congo." Pastor Joseph invited her to the crusade, and so both her and her husband were a blessing to us at the worship time. Other worship teams came forward, and we had a great time in the Lord, and the rain held off for the most part until I finished the message just as it was beginning to get dark.

On that day, Saturday, and on Sunday the finale, fewer came forward for salvation decisions, but many pressed in for healing prayers, and it was a magnificent time in the Kingdom of God.

The power of God present on the platform on Sunday, the final day of the crusade, was beyond anything I had experienced in the Congo. On the platform were seated many of the top pastors and bishops from the Goma area, along with their wives, along with our team, Pastor Joseph and his wife. So there was certainly a double portion anointing just from the dedicated servants of the Lord who were sitting behind me to cheer me on in the Spirit. As I gave the message on "The power in the blood of Jesus", again I felt like at times I would not be able to stand, like I was being overwhelmed by the unseen power of God.

People from Goma were packed into the street going both to my right and left, as well as in the church directly in front.

As I gave the altar call for people to come forward, I kept looking to the top of the small mountain to the right, thinking for sure this would be the day I would see the angels, and to the left to the top of the smoking Mt. Nyiragongo, thinking that would be the place that Jesus would manifest. To my disappointment, the Lord did not open my spiritual eyes that day, so I didn't see either, but again I felt like the anointing on the meeting was so great that surely someone was given the sight to see the angels and Jesus. By the time I had finished praying for the people who came forward, it was getting dark and the time to end the Goma crusade had now come.

As I have learned over the years of preaching crusades in Africa, the last night is always bittersweet, as it is so good to be riding the wave of the power of the Lord as it builds over the course of the week, but it is also good to come to the end to be able to rest and rejoice in seeing what God had accomplished. The spiritual battles and warfare in a setting such as Goma, and all through Africa for that matter, are so intense, a person needs to take a break from them and rest up at times.

And so as darkness enveloped the scene, we descended the platform and immediately were ushered into the pastor's car and headed back to the Cap Kivu Hotel. My heart was beating rapidly, and I had an overwhelming urge to cry. It was a cry for mercy and grace for the precious saints of Goma, those who had suffered so much over the years at the hands of rebels who had nothing on their minds but to exploit and steal, kill, and destroy. And a cry for those who had come forward to make decisions, and to ask for prayers for healing, that the Lord would hear their cry as well, and answer them in their time of need. As we arrived back at the Cap Kivu for the last night before departure, all the team gathered in the dining patio to relax and decompress, and we all shared in some great recollections as we devoured our meals of chicken and chips with hot tea. It was a time we could all rejoice in praising God for all He had done the last week.

The next morning came in bright and clear, and the day was the clearest of all the days yet that we had been in Goma; we could easily see to the other side of Lake Kivu, as if to almost be able to reach out and touch the mountains on the other side of the lake, which were in reality several kilometers away. The mountains surrounding the lake are home to some very rare species of gorillas, and I longed for the day when we would have time to go look at all those beautiful side attractions, as it would surely enhance for us the glory of God's creation. Sadly, we were scheduled to head back to Kigali about eleven that morning, with the church "translation" bus scheduled to pick us up at the hotel, clear customs at Gisenyi, Rwanda, and then on back to Kigali to catch the flight to Nairobi.

As I was drinking a cup of hot tea and milk about nine that morning, I received a phone call from Pastor Isaiah asking, "Would you be willing to meet with Prophetess Deborah this morning and pray for he?" "Yes," I replied, "but have her to come quickly as we are going to be leaving in a couple of hours, and I want to be sure to have time to pray with her." About an hour later Prophetess Deborah showed up with her Assistant Pastor and her oldest son, a young man about sixteen years of age. I met them in the dining patio, then motioned to them to follow me, "Let's go us to my room where it will be private and quiet." And so we all went up to the room as I knew this was going to be an exciting encounter with the Lord. Since meeting the Prophetess at her church that first day in Goma, I had learned from some of the pastors that she had a very unusual history.

Prophetess Deborah was a strikingly beautiful lady who had a regal air of elegance and confidence about her, and yet at the same time she was very humble. Besides being a Prophetess for the one true God, her appearance belied the behind the scenes story that was so amazing. She was a former Muslim who had come out of Islam and then became a pastor of her own church, but in addition to that, her husband was an imam in a local Goma mosque, and he still served in that capacity. By the grace of God, however, he had given her the freedom to pursue her new found faith in Jesus, and he had also granted her permission to raise their six children as Christian. As she stood before me with her pastor on one side and her son on the other, I anointed them all with oil and then began to pray and prophesy over her.

As I touched her forehead and then began to speak, she quickly got down on her knees as an act of humility, and also she could sense this was going to be a powerful encounter with the living God. As I began to pray for her, she began to shake, and the Holy Spirit took over and the prophetic words just came bubbling out. The Lord says, "You have been appointed for a time such as this. I have raised you up to be a leader of the people of God in this city, and your testimony, your faith walk, is a harbinger of what the Lord will do with many in Goma. They will see your walk, and they will know that the one true God has been in their midst, and they will desire to know Him as they watch you. Even your husband will come to know and serve the one true God. Your walk of faith is also a harbinger of the season I am bringing to Goma. No longer will there be a spirit of death and destruction over Goma, but I have now ushered in a season of peace and stability, a time for prosperity that will last for forty years! Listen to the words of the prophet, for I have honored their labor and their diligence in this place."

As I finished praying over her, she remained on her knees for several minutes, as a breathtaking stillness enveloped the room.

Slowly she got back to her feet, tears streaming from her eyes, and she said to me in her broken English, "I am very happy!" I replied back to her, "Yes, I am very happy as well, and the Lord, He is very happy, too!" What made the encounter even more amazing was that very morning, while reading the Bible through from Genesis to Revelation, I had read chapter five of Judges, which is the song of Deborah and Barak after they had defeated the enemies of Israel. Sister Jael had enticed Sisera, the leader of the enemy army, into her tent, where she drove a stake through his temple, as if to put an exclamation point on the finish of the battle. Then the last verse of Judges chapter five ends this way, *"Thus let all Your enemies perish, O Lord! But let those who love Him be like the sun when it comes out in full strength. So the land had rest for forty years."* (Judges 5:31)

As Prophetess Deborah and her team said their goodbyes to me and departed for their church, I knew God had spoken, and His word had truly been powerful, and the timing was perfect. Surely a time of prosperity and stability had come to Goma and North Kivu, and possibly as that area becomes stabilized, all of eastern Congo and the regions beyond will stabilize as well. The prophecy about forty years of rest really resonated in my spirit, and I believe that is what the Lord has for Goma as well. Only time will tell. But I was humbled and pleased to be a part of it, to see the difference that had come over the city in the two years since the King Jehoshaphat prophetic word, and I will be watching intently in the years to come, to see if the prophetic word spoken over Deborah comes to pass. By the grace of God, if she has anything to do with it, it surely will.

At promptly eleven o'clock the church minibus pulled up, and the three brothers who were going with us to Kigali, along with another car with the Pastor Joseph and his wife, rolled out of the parking lot of the Cap Kivu for the last time. I took one last look at the beautiful Lake Kivu, the mountains beyond, and the hotel and surroundings, and said to the Lord, "Lord, if it is Your will, let me come back to this city to minister again, to follow up on the prophetic word You gave." And so we left Goma in the hands of the Lord and the able pastors He has raised up to be guardians of that city.

We also left brother Richard behind as well, he was going to stay behind in Goma for a few days and do some more teaching at Pastor Joseph's church, and he also wanted to go back into Goma prison another time. We made it through the port of entry and customs in about an hour, and were on into Gisenyi and into the Rwandan countryside by one in the afternoon, right on schedule to make Kigali by four to be ready to board the plane.

After a couple hours of travel we were back near the village alongside the highway where we had stopped the week before on the way to Goma, and we were all in agreement the samosas had been good, so we should try them again a second time. So we bought a bag of samosas, and a round of sodas, and got back into the van and took off down the road. Life couldn't get any better than this, flying through the Rwandan countryside, headed home after a tremendous victory battling for the Lord!

After downing two or three samosas and the soda, however, life didn't seem quite so good; my stomach began to get a bit queasy, and by the time we got to the airport on the outskirts of Kigali, I was very happy to get out of the minibus and back on firm ground again. I thought, "I'll surely be okay, I just need to stop moving and take it easy, after I digest these samosas life will be good again." We had some time in the terminal before the plan departed, so Ronnie and Pastor Isaiah and I had a strong cup of coffee in the coffee shop next to the terminal, as we had an hour or so to kill before going through the terminal to the boarding gate. I thought surely the coffee would settle my stomach, but to no avail.

By the time we passed through the final checkpoint to the boarding gate, I was beginning to feel like I was in a tremendous battle with my stomach, and for now it was winning. I was also beginning to feel a bit faint, and I knew I was in for a time of sickness, as I had been down this road before in Africa, thinking back to the year 2012 when I battled sickness for a night, also in Goma. When we passed through the checkpoint to the boarding lounge, we were scanned by a nurse who had a laser scanner. She was checking for anyone with a rise in temperature that might indicate the presence of the Ebola virus, as it was the height of the Ebola crisis that had erupted in West Africa. The Ebola epidemic had taken many lives in West African nations, but so far had not surfaced in East African nations. But as a result of the scare, all the airports in East Africa were now scanning every passenger of every flight just as a precautionary measure.

The flight to Nairobi was scheduled to be a two hour flight, and by the time we boarded at six that evening, Rwanda time, I was starting to feel very sick, to the point of wondering if I was going to make it to Nairobi without heaving my samosas. When I got on the plane and it prepared for takeoff, it didn't take me long to find out; within ten minutes after getting up in the air I was in the lavatory vomiting up everything that I had taken in that day. After about the third trip to the lavatory, the stewardesses were beginning to take notice of me, and offered me blankets, sodas, and even the promise of medical attention when we got to Kenyatta Airport in Nairobi.

The third time into the lavatory, I was on my knees leaning over the stool, sweating profusely after I had just vomited again, and then the Holy Spirit spoke to me the prophetic word given by my Prophetess back in America before I left, when she said, "The Lord is taking you to a higher place of warfare than you have ever been before, and it's not going to be pretty!" I thought about myself leaned over the toilet in that little lavatory, wrenching my guts out, and thought, "She was right about that, this certainly isn't very pretty."

CHAPTER 18

NAIROBI

What was supposed to be a routine two hour flight turned into three hours, as the plane ahead of us had landing gear problems that delayed us for half an hour, and then when we got on the ground we were delayed another half hour from unknown causes before we could exit the plane. By that time the stewardesses were convinced I needed medical care, they probably thought I had Ebola, and they offered several times to get me medical care. I just kept saying to them, in a half delirious state of consciousness, "I think it's just those samosas", not really knowing for sure if it was that or just a good battle of spiritual warfare in the light of the prophecy.

By the grace of God we finally got off the plane, but the next obstacle was in the line at the visa entry point into Kenya, where we all had to go through another laser temperature scan before we could get our visa into Kenya. I could barely stand at that point, so I asked brother Ronnie and Pastor Isaiah to pray for me, as I felt sure I had a full blown fever. I didn't want to be held up in Nairobi quarantine for twenty one days waiting to find out if I had Ebola virus, when I was almost certain it was the samosas that had caused the problem.

As I was standing in the line for the temperature scan, I just kept praying, "Lord, let me pass through this scan, I just need a good night's rest and I will be okay." God must have heard my prayer, for when I got to the nurse with the scanner, she did a quick scan of me and motioned me to go on through to the visa application line. I thought to myself, "God, You certainly have mercy on Your servant, thank you, Jesus. " However, my troubles for that night were far from over. Two other much larger airplanes from Europe had just landed at the same time as our smaller plane, and there was a huge bottleneck of people waiting in the lines to get their visas. About three to four hundred people, we were standing in four lines that were moving at a snail's pace, so I knew this was going to take another hour or more. At least I was done vomiting for the time being, but I still was too weak to stand, so I just got down on one knee and pushed and pulled my baggage through the line, as it slowly moved up to the visa purchase counter.

The visa purchases went smoothly, but another hour went by before we got a cab secured and I was in the back seat of the cab, headed with Ronnie for the hotel and what I hoped would be a good night's sleep. I instantly fell asleep in the cab, and didn't even know whether we encountered a jam or not, but it seemed like no time we were at the hotel. After securing our rooms, it was almost midnight by the time I crawled into bed.

Unfortunately, however, the battle was still not over. I spent the next three or four hours back and forth to the toilet with severe cramps, diarrhea, and even some more vomiting, as the enemy was not done with me, he was getting back at me for all the good work done for the kingdom in Goma. Finally, about three in the morning, I settled in for a good sleep and slept until ten the next morning, when I got a call on the room phone from Larry,

Pastor Luke's brother, who was waiting for Ronnie and I down in the lobby.

I had asked Larry to get us some prices on travel fares and tickets to the Maasai Mara Wildlife Refuge to go see the big animals, so he was down in the lobby waiting for us to come down so he could tell us what he found out. He gave us the tour prices for two days on the Mara, with an overnight stay in a safari camp, all for the good price of four hundred and fifty dollars, everything included. I said to him, "Thank you for your work brother, I really appreciate it, but I don't think I can make it. I have been sick ever since we left Rwanda, and I didn't get hardly any good sleep last night, so I think I am going to pass on the offer. We'll just hang around Nairobi this week and then get ready to fly out on Friday night, back to home, sweet home in Kansas." Brother Ronnie was feeling of the same inclination, while although he was feeling good physically, his funds were running low and he didn't think he could come up with the money required for the two day excursion. So we had to cancel out on the trip, but we both pledged to take it in on the next trip to Kenya.

That first day in Nairobi I spent in and out of bed, drinking some hot tea, watching some soccer on the television, and praying for God to heal me and strengthen me for the rest of the week. Ronnie was enjoying the sights and sounds of Nairobi, and in addition, there was a chicken and chips local restaurant right next door that he was enjoying. They served up an awesome platter of chicken and chips for three hundred Kenya shillings, or about four dollars. That was a great relief on the budget after the overly priced entrees at the Cap Kivu in Goma. We were in a hotel right in the middle of a bustling neighborhood in Buruburu, a heavily populated enclave of Nairobi about thirty minutes from the airport, and twelve kilometers from the center of the city. After a day of rest and relaxation, my stomach finally started to settle down, and that night I even took in a light supper of rice and vegetables in the hotel restaurant.

The next day I was feeling even stronger, and decided to venture out with Larry and Ronnie to a nearby Tuskys Supermart within a couple of blocks of the hotel. We went there to look at the wares, and buy a few gifts for our people at home. After shopping for a while, we stopped into a small diner connected to the main shopping center. We each ordered a fresh fruit smoothie, the fruit juice smoothies in Nairobi are to die for, they are so sweet and natural compared to what we can get in the states.

As I was sitting enjoying my smoothie, I struck up a conversation with a lady at the table beside me; I had seen her in the same hotel we were staying, she was with several young ladies that appeared to be college students. As she introduced herself, it proved that my hunch was right. She was a college professor from the Netherlands, with a group of students in tow, and they were in Nairobi to do some social work canvassing and data collection in the Mathare slum, one of the largest and poorest slums in Nairobi, very similar to Kibera. The collection of several slums that go under the name of Mathare are said to have a population of about half a million individuals, and all live in wretched, six foot by eight foot sheet metal shanties, surviving on less than a dollar a day.

As we were visiting, another student came in to join her teacher, and she was introduced to me as Ellen, a very pretty young lady in her mid-twenties. She was the author of a book that had just recently been published, in which she interviewed many people from the Mathare slum, telling their stories in their own words of what brought them to Mathare, and how they managed to survive in that place. After we chatted about her book and research for a few minutes, she then asked me, "What are you doing in Kenya?" I replied, "I am an evangelist from America, and my team and I have been here for almost a month, conducting pastor training meetings and crusades in Kenya and Congo." "Wow," she said, "So, you went over to the Congo, that's very interesting." As we conversed, I got around to asking her about her faith and what she believed about Jesus Christ.

She said," I believe that Jesus was a good man, a prophet, but I don't hold him above any other of the great moral leaders in the history of the world."

I quickly discerned that she was totally steeped in the secular humanistic philosophy that had swept through most of the European countries the last generation. She believed that the solution to all of mankind's problems, including the grinding poverty of Mathare, lie within the genius of man's education and intellect. I asked her, "If I prayed for Jesus to reveal Himself to you, and show you that He is real, would you pray that prayer with me?" She said. "Yes, I would pray that with you!"

So I took her to another table away from the crowd, and as I talked to her before we began to pray, she exclaimed, "Wow, I am feeling very excited, is that normal?" I said, "Yes, that is normal, for the Holy Spirit of God is touching you, and the Lord Himself is going to reveal Himself to you in some way, just as He is revealing Himself to you right now through me. Do you think this is just a coincidence that the Lord put me in your path this day at this moment in time?" She conceded, "No, I'm sure it is for some purpose and not just a coincidence."

And so I held her hand and prayed for Jesus to reveal Himself to her, and I asked the Lord to bless her life and the sales of her book, that He would show her favor as a result of the encounter with Him today. As I ended the prayer, her countenance had lifted and gotten much brighter, and she was just about breathless, as she repeated again, "Wow, this is so exciting!" Shortly after that the students and their teacher left the diner, but I'm certain I will see the young lady again in Glory Land after our work on earth is done.

The Thursday of that week was to be the final day in Nairobi before we flew out on Friday, and Ronnie and I decided we would venture across town to eat at a famous safari restaurant called Carnivore. Carnivore is a favorite stop for all the foreign tourists, safari companies, and locals who just love a great meal in a very casual, yet beautiful atmosphere. I called my Nairobi friend, whose Christian name is Hope, the ex-Muslim who had gotten saved at the Kibera Crusade in 2011, to see if she wanted to meet us at Carnivore, and she said, "I would be delighted to do so, I'll meet you downtown and then take you in my car to Carnivore." So Ronnie and I got in a car with Larry who was going to take us downtown to meet Hope at a predetermined place in the heart of city center.

After meeting up with Hope, we took off for Carnivore, about another twenty minutes from the city center, and upon arriving found the place to be quite empty, but still with the great food and ambience nonetheless. The terrorist attacks across Kenya were having a devastating impact upon the tourism and safari industry as a whole, and places like Carnivore that depend so much on tourism, were struggling to stay alive. As we settled down to a table to eat, I had a pleasant conversation with Hope, and asked her, "How are you doing in your new found faith walk with Jesus?" She replied with a sparkle in her eye, "Oh, I love Jesus so much, He is everything to me. I just worry about the safety of my children, as we continue to get threats."

And truly Jesus does mean everything to her, as she has had to give up just about everything to walk with the Lord Jesus; all her belongings, her Muslim family, including her father who raised her, and not only that, she has had to conceal her identity and place of residence from her ex- husband, who did not take lightly her walking away from him and her Muslim faith.

By the time we finished eating our lunch, we were all stuffed to the maximum, so we sat and talked about plans for the future of the Gather the Outcasts Ministry. After praying over the plans, and saying goodbye to that great place for another year, we left the ambiance of Carnivore to go back out into the jam and noise of Nairobi. Hope took Ronnie and I down to the train station, to get on the five o'clock train that would take us back to Buruburu within about four block of our hotel. The train was an experience all in itself, it was old, rickety, and looked like it had been in service for about fifty years, which I don't doubt that it probably had, maybe since the British left Kenya over fifty years ago. After waiting for an hour for the train to leave the downtown station, we got to Buruburu in just over fifteen minutes, then we had to walk only about four blocks, so in all it was still faster than sitting in the jam.

The next day, Friday, was our departure day, and we were scheduled to be at the Uhuru Kenyatta International Airport at eight in the evening, two hours before the departure time at ten. The jam was light going in the direction of the airport, and we made it in plenty of time to have time to rest and relax before the flight. After an uneventful nine hour trip to Amsterdam, a rather fleeting two hour layover, we were late getting off to Detroit for the next leg of the journey, another eight hour flight. When we hit the ground in Detroit, we had just barely over an hour to get to our next flight to Kansas City, so it was a mad dash through the US Customs, pick up the bags, recheck of the bags, and then to the boarding gate for the last leg, the two hour flight to Kansas City.

It was an exhausting finish to the trip, not only from the mad dash at the end, and the overall twenty five hour duration, but also the loss of eight hours of time between the time of Nairobi and Kansas City. That jet lag always usually takes me at least a week to get over, and in the recuperation time I often times just hit the wall in the middle of the afternoon. I have to say when I got to Kansas City, I wanted to get down on my knees and kiss the earth, America looked so good to me. I didn't get down for fear I would be looked upon as a fool, but I was so thankful to be back in America, I just wanted to praise the Lord for the safe travel and all the great victories along the way. But while waiting for our ride to come pick us up outside the Kansas City Airport terminal, I did cry out to the Lord, "Bwana Asifiwe! Praise the Lord! Asante, Jesus. Thank you, Jesus!" Amen!

EPILOGUE

Kenya Orphanage Project

During the last two years' trips to Africa, the Lord has put in my heart a burden for the children of Africa. The prayer focus at the International House of Prayer in 2013, to pray for the children of Uganda, and then again in 2014 to see the plight of all the children of Kenya who were at the Malaba Crusade, has highlighted for me the needs of the children in Africa, many who are orphans and don't have proper food and clothing, or a place to call home.

At the same time this burden has been growing in me, the brethren of the church of Pastor Luke in Mumias have been praying and fasting for the Lord to move through Gather the Outcasts Ministry to provide for the orphan children in the Mumias area. His church has already been caring for and feeding many orphan children, this is not unusual in Africa. Just about all pastors and churches take responsibility for orphan children, but they want to provide for the children in greater measure by building a home for them.

In Kenya alone there are between two and three million orphan children, primarily due to the AIDS epidemic that swept through the country, beginning in the early 1990's, and still continuing today.

Kenya has the fourth highest HIV epidemic of all the African nations. Though the adult prevalence rate of infection has decreased dramatically in recent years, from the peak in 1996 of 10.5%, to 6.1% in 2012, the number of children left in the wake of this epidemic has overwhelmed the available social services of the country.

The vision given to the church, and to me, has coalesced at the same time to bring this vision to fruition in the present season. At the time of the writing of this book, the land for this Living Water Orphanage, which will provide a home for fifty orphan children, out in the country near Mumias, in far west Kenya, has been purchased and plans are going forward to get the orphanage built in the summer of 2015.

I pray that many who read the pages of this book will also feel the burden given to this Evangelist, and they would come alongside Gather the Outcasts Ministry to help provide for the homeless children of Kenya. If the Lord is moving on your heart to help with this project, please see the contact information at the back of this book. May God bless you for your care and love offering.

CONTACT INFORMATION:

Gather the Outcasts Ministry,Inc.

PO Box 92,

Norton, Ks. 67654

501(c)(3) Charitable Donation

email: pureprairie@hotmail.com

web: www.gathertheoutcasts.com